To Brenda,
one of our best students
and one of our finest
girls, Love,
R. D. R.

How
to Bring Up
2000
Teenagers

How to Bring Up 2000 Teenagers

Ralph Rutenber

Nelson-Hall/Chicago

LIBRARY OF CONGRESS CATALOGING IN PUBLICATION DATA

Rutenber, Ralph.
    How to bring up 2000 teenagers.

    Includes index.
    1. Adolescence. 2. Children—Management. I. Title.
HQ796.R87   649'.125   78–24060
    ISBN 0–88229–550–0

Manufactured in the United States of America

10   9   8   7   6   5   4   3   2   1

Contents

To Cleminette with love and admiration

Pages 45 and 47 have been transposed

1 The Second Question

Is there anything new to be said about teenagers? After all the articles? After all the books? After all the speeches and conferences? After all the fulsome praise and the savage criticism?

I think there is.

The psychologists, journalists, psychiatrists, sociologists, apologists, educators, clergymen, anthropologists, and sexologists; the youth adorers and the youth haters; those who are afraid that a harsh word will scrape the gauze from the butterfly's wings and it will never fly again; and those who believe that the answer to all problems is to take the young to the woodshed and give them a good thrashing—have all had their say. This onrush of expert and inexpert opinion; this spate of Deep Thoughts, Newest Solutions, Oldest Reactions, Future Shocks, Present Perfects, Past Imperfects, New Moralities, Old Imperatives, Lessons of Watergate, Counter Cultures, Greenings of America, and Falls of Rome have held the floor as long as I have been in the business of bringing up young people. We parents, teachers, and counselors have taken

1

our notes, read our assignments, and listened with hope and excitement for the Final Word, only to admit at last with Auden:

> And the nightingale is dumb,
> And the angel will not come.[1]

If the nightingale does not sing and the angel does not appear after all that the prophets have spoken, perhaps we should take a hard look at the prophets and search out some of the myths of our culture.

All high-minded people—and parents, teachers, and counselors are genuinely high-minded—have been asking the same question for the last fifty years: What can we do for young people? This is the shoe that keeps dropping.

The experts who tell us how badly we've done, or what we are now doing wrong, or what we ought to do, are trying to answer this question. The overworked parents, principals, headmasters, teachers, and counselors are trying to answer the same question in the tireless trudge of the everyday. We smile at the story of the housewife who, surveying the wreckage of the living room after her young children and their friends had been playing in it, remarked ruefully, "Sometimes I wish I had loved and lost!"

The answers we receive at any given time are distressingly similar, although there are always, thank God, dissenting voices. At the moment we are in the stage of Permissiveness Minus in the matter of discipline; i.e., we think maybe we have given in to young people too much in permitting them to do what they want to do, although we are certainly not going back to anything that might be labeled authoritarian. Permissiveness Plus is the overriding trend

---

[1] "Now the Leaves Are Falling Fast," from *W. H. Auden, Collected Poems,* edited by Edward Mendelson. Copyright © 1976, Random House, Inc.

in the school curriculum; i.e., we must give our students not only a choice between forty or fifty mini-courses on every conceivable subject but must also provide, in the words of three dozen experts who wrote *The Greening of the High School,* the "provision of alternative and non-traditional styles of education," "real world experience" —whatever that is—during the high school day to supplement the strictly academic, and, to quote the author of *Future Shock,* programs like "traffic control" or "driving a delivery truck," for which educational credit should be granted.

A year from now someone else will suddenly suggest that the parents should give each child twenty, not twenty-one, whacks on the rear to instill in him responsible self-discipline, or will write a book to prove that four years of Sanskrit is the real answer to that endless groping for the perfect curriculum, both liberal arts and vocational, both challenging and easy, both geared to the slow student and to the brilliant one, both, both, both—and....

What can we give our young people? Shall we try twenty whacks on the behind, not twenty-one, and four years of Sanskrit in high school?

And of course there are always a few parents who will say, "What can we do for our children? Why, that's easy. Give them a car, pretty clothes (if they'll wear them), summers at the beach—and whatever else we can afford."

In dealing with 2000 adolescents, both boys and girls, I learned that there is another question, a second shoe that we seem to be afraid to drop. It is a simple question, as obvious as the one around which we have built for so many years our relationship to young people as parents or teachers.

It did not come to me on the Road to Damascus. There was no light that shone about me, no voice from heaven.

There were thirty-three girls in a bankrupt school we

had just taken over, six boarders and twenty-seven day pupils. Five of the boarders were seniors. There were three old buildings on an acre of land in the middle of a city. The cook had just quit, and my wife had gone down to the kitchen. Two girls who had heard the news met me in the hall. "Sir, what can we do for you?" they asked.

This book is not the story of that school and how it grew. It is the story of a way of bringing up young people based on two questions rather than only one. Both questions are equally important: What can we the adult world of parent, teacher, and administrator give to young people, and, What can young people, our children and our students, give to the adult world?

It is the second question that has long since been forgotten by parents and teachers. We have developed two classes in our society, the givers—us, the recipients—young people. Although we believe and rightly that it is "more blessed to give than to receive" (and blessed means happy, joyful), we have denied that blessedness to our children. We have said in effect: You can have the excitement of giving and of being needed when you are grown up. Meanwhile, please let us have the pleasure and satisfaction of doing things for you, and don't forget to be grateful for all that we give you.

The recipients have received but they have not been grateful. "My child is a wonderful accepter," a mother said to me bitterly when her daughter's grades began to drop in her junior year through lack of effort, "but when it comes to giving . . ." What could she expect? You cannot be a recipient for sixteen years and suddenly become a giver overnight.

They have not been grateful. I remember a businessman and his wife with an attractive daughter, their only child. "I guess we spoil her," Mr. Banks said to me once smiling, "but we sure are having a wonderful time doing it." There was no doubt that both statements were true, but their daughter Connie learned the pleasures of giving in the MacDuffie community, and she turned against her parents' philosophy.

She came to see me in her junior year to discuss college.

"Sir, may I see you about college?"

"Sure, sit down."

"I want to go to some college in California," she said definitely.

I was surprised. "Well," I said, "that's fine. Are your parents willing to have you go so far away?"

"They are very unhappy about it," she said, "but they are the reason I want to go. I want to be as far away from them as possible. Oh, I know it sounds terrible, and I do love them, but you know, sir, as well as I, that when I came to this school I was a spoiled brat. They've always given me everything in the world, and it's taken me three years to break away from them and find myself. They don't understand it. They still want me to be Mommy's and Daddy's little darling. They are terribly hurt that I am so insistent on going to California. I try to explain that I still love them, but I am tired of having everything done for me. I have told them that I have enough things, and I don't want to go to the shore this summer. I want to get a job, maybe helping somebody. I feel so selfish. Can you explain it to them without hurting their feelings? I'm *not* going to college in New England."

"I'll do my best," I said, "but I can't guarantee that I won't hurt their feelings."

"Thank you, sir."

There is something in healthy human nature that rebels against receiving and receiving and receiving—and never having a chance to give. There is something in healthy human nature that does not want to be forever kneeling. "The hand that feeds us is in some danger of being bitten," say Emerson. It is an angry bite. It says: "I know what you are doing for me, and what pride and satisfaction you are getting from it. But where do I find my pride and satisfaction? On my knees, forever thanking you?"

Most adolescents, wrapped in the generous arms of the economy and cradled up to the early twenties from hard labor in any form except school work, are looking desperately for ways to escape the clinging web of dependence. They will not thank you for drawing it tighter, no matter how ungrateful you think they are.

The mother who has "devoted" her life to her children is hurt and bewildered when they turn on her and snap, "I didn't ask to be born." What they really mean is: "I didn't ask to be the continual recipient of your largesse, to be forever eating at the shining table that you have so lavishly set for me. There are times when I feel so inferior and unneeded that I would like to smash the table to pieces and throw the plates against the wall which you have dusted with your loving hands."

Long before the bricks tore through the windows of the alabaster cities and the universities cowered under seventy-times-seven days of rage; long before Tom Hayden wrote "Two, Three, Many Columbias"; long before Mario Savio and the sit-ins at Berkeley (I was there five years later listening to a man still urging his audience to "burn it down"), young people, whether they knew it or not, were begging for the pleasure and power of giving, instead of eternally receiving. Oh, they didn't protest the golden stream of gifts and services that parents and society showered upon them. Nobody said, "Don't give me a T.V. set or a car or a healthy allowance to spend on myself." But nobody said thank you very hard either. Whether they expressed it with the "NonThink" violence of the SDS primitives or the pious sonorities of the Younger Clergymen's Club; whether in the forties and fifties they could even find a flag around which they could rally except the banner of "getting ahead"—the fact remains that then as now and always the *receivers* of our affluence and over-protection wanted also to *give*.

First prize for the Easy Solution of the Youth Problem goes to the persuasive proposition that if young people were only a "part of the decision-making process," the generation gap would close quietly like the doors of an elevator and the lion and the lamb (depending on your point of view) would slide serenely to the very top floor in each other's embrace.

The middle-aged youthies who infested our campuses during the revolt of the sixties; the advocates of genuflection who spiced their droop by aligning themselves with youthful protest and even violence; the earnest young thinkers who announced breathlessly that a New Morality was afoot (or abed)—all urged us to counter the alienation of youth by putting them on the Board of Directors of industry, and especially on the Board of Trustees of our colleges, universities, and schools.

I am convinced that young people do not want to be adults. I have not found many who have been willing to sit in the seat of power when it meant that they would have to punish their own peer group for breaking the rules they themselves had made.

They want their opinions known—yes. They want to be able to tell you what they think and what they would like to do, and what they would like you to do. They are glad to have you "consider" their ideas, and they are rightfully indignant if you tear down their sense of dignity and self-worth by telling them they are "too young" or "too immature." They are young adults, sons and daughters of Janus, the two-headed god. One head looks wistfully back to childhood and the other looks confidently ahead to adulthood. They need an adult structure against which to test themselves and their ideas, and as young adults they need the responsibilities they can handle—as soon as they show they can handle them. But they do not want to be an integral part of decisions that exact penalties on their friends. Nor did we at their age.

So the administration "gives," be it in the home or the school. But discontent and, in the sixties, violence only increase in direct proportion, it would seem, to the privileges bestowed on the dissenting and demanding young. Student councils in the turbulent sixties became pressure vehicles against the educational establishment, just as well-meaning family councils became a means to more privileges with the family car and later hours with dates.

I wrote a jingle for a convention of educators who were wrestling, as I was, with the pressures of the student-activist movement:

The Applicant

I want a school whose standards are as high as
    they can be.
Of course I want the homework to be light.
From regulations I would like to be completely free,
Except the ones that I consider right.

I hope the Student Council isn't just a bunch of finks,
Upholding every petty regulation.
A Student Council's job, unless the system
    really stinks,
Is getting things from the Administration.

I hope your teachers make the work immediately clear.
I trust your grades are only pass or fail.
I think the most important thing is just to be sincere.
Is that enough to get me into Yale?

"Privileges bestowed"—that is the important phrase. What can we do for you—to keep you off our backs? What can we do for you—to give us some peace in the home or the school? What can we do for you that makes *us* feel important and generous and successful?

It has not been recorded that any young person was ever spoiled into maturity (or scolded, jeered at, or neglected into becoming a strong and responsible adult). You cannot give enough to the demanding young when you are the bestower—enough privileges and concessions and material things, at least.

As I have said, they need an adult structure against which to test themselves; but they have nothing but contempt for parents or teachers who cave in at their requests or demands.

An earnest young teacher comes into my office at a boys' school.

"I don't know what to do with Staples," he says. "He's very fresh and is constantly disrupting the class. I can't do a thing with him. What would you do if you told a boy to sit down and he wouldn't?"

What can I tell him that doesn't sound smug? That when I tell a boy to sit down he sits down? That would only lower him still further in his own eyes.

I try to give him some insight into the situation. "Act as if you expected to be obeyed," I say. "Pitch your voice low, but with an edge to it. Talk to him privately and try to get a better relationship." I have a feeling it isn't going to work. I hope I am not conveying this to him, but I probably am.

A few unhappy weeks later, he is back in my office, anxious and upset.

"Please, Ralph, will you talk to Staples? The class is responding to him. It's getting out of hand."

"Paul, it's going to make you look weak if I have to take over. Are you sure you really want me to?"

We discuss it, but he is adamant. "Please talk to him, It can't be any worse than it is now."

I call Staples in, a new eighth grader, thirteen years old. I'm not about to waste any time.

"I understand from Mr. Billings that you are disruptive in class and insubordinate to the point of defying him when he tells you to sit down and be quiet. What have you got to say about it?"

His answer is immediate. "If he isn't man enough to make me behave, why should I keep quiet?"

"If he isn't man enough...." I have never forgotten the phrase.

They want us to be "man enough", that is, adults.

To list the many ways in which young people can be involved in the adult world of home and school and society is impossible until the relationships between young people and older people, the ways in which they live together in the community, are clearly defined. Giving to the adult community presupposes a certain kind of community and certain methods of bringing up young people that make them want to give, since a gift is something bestowed and not demanded.

And let us not forget that a contribution does not have to be a planned action. It may just as well grow out of an unexpected situation that prompts a display of certain qualities, like courage, that have a profound effect on the community.

2 The Community of Expectation

I am sure that no one is so romantic as to suppose that the headmaster of a boarding school sits happily in his office while a long line of boys or girls comes filing in, bleating, "Sir, what can I do for you today?"

The relationships between the student and the headmaster (I am using the term headmaster conveniently to stand for the adult generation and especially for those in authority: parents, teachers, counselors, etc.) are rugged and often abrasive. Dealing with the young on a day-to-day basis is not for the sentimental. The jam in their hearts is likely to show up on their faces. Affection cannot be too obvious, especially in the school situation, lest one lose his or her union card in Young People's Local 666. But it is there and comes out sometimes in peculiar ways.

I remember the sophomore who lived in a dormitory where the "in" thing was to cut the school down and announce loudly that one certainly wasn't coming back next year. One was going to some school, public or private, where the rules weren't so petty (a petty rule is one that you don't like); where one didn't have to study so hard, etc., etc.

11

Lee was passing me in the corridor of the school building. She veered a little to one side so that she wouldn't be heard and said: "Sir, I have some news that I think will please you. I want you to know that I'm coming back next year, but please don't tell anybody."

"Little one," I said, "I'm very pleased, and I promise you I won't tell a soul."

I smiled. She beamed, and went on. I had received the Accolade.

Somewhat more blunt, but no less complimentary, was the girl who had been in the school well over a year. She came into my office and said: "Sir, I just wanted to tell you that I have decided you're not a phony. For a long time I thought you were a phony, but you're really not. I thought you'd like to know."

Who wouldn't? Phony was the big word that year. Not to be a phony was almost like being Rod McKuen.

I told her I was indeed glad that she had decided I wasn't a phony. I assured her that she was a pretty real person herself. We parted fine friends.

Occasionally, from the very beginning, a girl is sufficiently sure of herself to let her feelings be known at once.

She didn't look like an especially strong person when I came up to the third floor on opening day. The mother was unpacking, and it seemed to me that the girl could be helping her mother more than she was.

She even looked a little helpless, and I made a mental note that the mother was probably overprotective. But certainly nice. I remembered the interview.

"Hello, Jean," I said, "how are you coming?"

She smiled. "My mother's coming fine," she said. "She's doing all the work."

"Don't you have an irresistible urge to help her?" I asked.

"I might," she said, "but it would run right into her irresistible urge to do it all by herself."

Jean was a sophomore. She was a pretty blonde, with a rather fragile look about her, as if she could not face anything too harsh or difficult.

She picked up a dress from the trunk and hung it up.

"Look, sir," she said, "I'm helping. Aren't you pleased with me?"

She said it as if she were amused, as if I were a little boy who had memorized a speech about being helpful. She was completely at ease. She was kidding me. I decided she wasn't as helpless as she looked. I also decided I liked her.

She was one of the girls who shaped the school in the early years.

Communities may be formed self-consciously, but the individual relationships cannot be self-conscious. I knew in my mind's eye the kind of school I wanted to have, and I learned by experience that the students wanted to be needed, and therefore to give as well as receive. But I never expected them to make their feelings verbal, and they never expected me, I am sure, to give a Friday morning talk on This Is a Great School Because We're All so Wonderful.

Have you ever been in a home where the father was trying to be a "real pal" to his son? So he takes him fishing, and he plays catch with him, and he asks him how school is going, and is anything bothering him. I know of one such family where, after many years of self-conscious togetherness, the boy finally said to his father, in a despairing tone, "Dad, you sure do try." He probably added under his breath, "Why the hell don't you leave me alone?"

I felt sorry for the father, who wanted to be close to his son. It is a worthy, proper, and important ideal. Every good father has it. But every good father has to learn that young people, even in their own homes, will flee from the parent or mentor who too obviously wants to Do Them Good. They are uncomfortable with oversolicitude, embarrassed by emotion unless they are used to it, and resentful of the feeling of being under someone's wing.

Some friends of mine who went to a therapy institute described to me earnestly how members of the group of both sexes stood naked in a swimming pool and held up one of their number on their hands above the water to give her a sense of utter security and group affection. I doubt that it would ever work with teenagers. Someone would giggle self-consciously in the face of such ponderous solemnity; someone else would shift her grip; the perfect balance would be broken; and the uplifted recipient of group support would no doubt fall back into the water amidst screams of laughter.

Relationships in a community grow out of the experience of the individuals in it: the situations in which they find themselves, and the people whom they meet every day. They do not grow from a lecture on Relationships, a theory of the community, or a philosophy of social dynamics. They cannot be programmed—B. F. Skinner to the contrary notwithstanding.

The home and the school are the enclaves where young people have the greatest chance to be both participants and observers in the process of growing up. The advantages of the home are obvious, but the school has advantages even greater in some areas, especially for high school students. The fifteen-year-old will be the only girl her own age in the home, but in the school community she will be living with many girls who are fifteen, along with younger ones of fourteen, and older ones of sixteen, seventeen and sometimes eighteen. And she is living with many adults of both sexes and of varying ages, who can view her with more objectivity than her parents, and to whom she can talk with far more frankness in most cases.

The second question is one of the great omissions in modern orthodoxies about bringing up young people, but there are others almost as devastating which will be taken up in this book.

One of these is the concept of the heroic. We have been so inhibited by the dogmatic and perpetually asserted myth that young people today have only a few heroes—all dead—that we have left out of our training almost any reference to courage, daring, or sacrifice, as if we were somehow embarrassed to talk about such qualities.

We advise our children in the words of an Ogden Nash couplet:

> Hark, it's midnight, children dear.
> Duck! Here comes another year![1]

You can't be too careful. Don't stick your neck out. Duck. There's no use in being unpopular. You can't change people's opinions. Politicians have always been crooked. Don't take a chance. Duck.

We have given our boys a faint tinge of the heroic, although the soft throat of our sophistication gags at the word. They may play football, a sport I have coached in boys' school. Something of the courage of battling against odds, of refusing to be beaten, of endlessly going back to the line and facing stronger men who have already proved themselves able to brush you aside and push your head in the dirt comes through, vicariously at least, to the spectators at a football game.

Hemingway's young bullfighter in *The Sun Also Rises*, knocked down fifteen times by the ex-prizefighter, and still trying to fight from the floor, is a modern illustration of guts, although the surrounding atmosphere could hardly be considered heroic.

But these are rather obvious examples of physical

---

[1] From "Good Riddance But Now What," in *Bed Riddance* (Little, Brown and Company, 1970).

courage. They tell us little about the world of moral courage, which is waiting to be invaded. And they involve men, as if women were forever barred from heroism because they weren't football players or bullfighters.

The only heroism Hemingway allows Brett Ashley in his book is her decision "not to be one of those bitches that ruins children." She is talking about her nineteen-year-old lover, whom she has given up to his beloved sport, bullfighting, not without many tears and a string of martinis.

The very first week I was at MacDuffie, I learned the subtle cultural pressures on girls.

I had, very mildly I thought, reproved a girl for talking in the library. That afternoon I got a call from her mother. Her tone was sharp.

"Mr. Rutenber," she said, "Debbie came home from school today very, very upset."

"Oh, really," I said, in complete innocence. "What was the trouble?"

"Why, the bawling out she got from you. The poor girl was in tears."

"I didn't bawl your daughter out," I protested. "I hardly spoke to her all day. It must have been somebody else."

"It was you, Mr. Rutenber," she said, as if I had almost beaten her child to death. "Didn't you speak to her about talking in the library?"

It was my turn to protest. "I did speak to her, Mrs. Burns, but by no stretch of the imagination could it be called a bawling out. I didn't even raise my voice."

She ignored the explanation. "You came from a boys' school, Mr. Rutenber. If you had talked that way to Debbie's brother, I wouldn't have minded at all. But Debbie is a girl!"

One would have thought she was describing some new, hardly named species: a delicate, ethereal creature barely sturdy enough to remain on earth. Actually Debbie was a strong, vital girl, with energy bursting out all over. And ego to match. I always wished I had had her for more than a year.

Several weeks later, when I went up to see Frank Boyden at Deerfield (all young headmasters made a pilgrimage to Frank Boyden), he said to me:

"Just what do you expect to do in a girls' school, Ralph?"

My answer by then was at least partially formulated, thanks to Debbie's mother.

"I want to run a girls' school just like a boys' school," I told him. "I want the same emphasis on the ability to take it, on courage, on picking yourself off the floor and starting all over again."

A few months later I would have added: "Although a great many women told me I would find girls devious when I switched from boys' schools to girls', I have found them as frank, honest, generous, and friendly as I found boys. Why do women run down their own sex?"

Whatever is in this book on *How to Bring Up 2000 Teenagers* applies to boys and girls equally, although most of the case histories will be from a girls' school because I have been a headmaster there.

Our timorous communities of home and school have been scared to death to present young people with the situations that would give them ego-strength, or to take advantage of these situations when they arise. (I use the word "situations" rather than the term "life situations," the beloved cliché of modern educators. Any situation involving a living person is a life situation. Life situations happen in the kitchen of a home or the corridor of a school, even in a library, just as often and as forcefully as they do in driving a truck or building a wall.)

The home and the school are crammed with situations, sometimes amounting to crises, usually much more mundane, that the skillful parent or teacher can use to teach the excitement of giving or the satisfaction of acting with courage.

The expectation of the adult community is crucial to the actions of young people. Expectation and affection are the two most important elements in bringing up teenagers. Here again, we are faced with the timidity of adults who have been afraid to follow their own antennae in the face of the closed ranks of orthodox commentators on the Generation Gap. Parents especially have been led to believe that their children do not wish to hear their views on any subject, and Margaret Mead even asserts with her customary vigor and dogmatism that adults today have nothing to teach young people; that the young people should in fact be teaching the adults. I want to be there when Dr. Mead sits down to learn about anthropology from a teenager.

We know from our own experience that all of us tend to follow the expectations of the community, even in trivia. Where is the corporate director who will appear at a Board Meeting on a hot day in slacks, an open shirt, and no coat?

More than we realize, we are what other persons—especially the ones we love and respect—expect us to be. If the adult world does not have "great expectations" for young people, they will take their cue from the peer group.

By great expectations, I most emphatically do not mean the pressure to achieve spectacular results which will give the parents a vicarious feeling of success. The pressure to get all As if you only try; to be first in this activity or that; to "shine" in a way that will give your parents a chance to boast about you—are self-centered expectations that much too often do not take into account the person's limitations, and are likely to produce a tense child with a battered self-image.

I am talking about the expectations that a person will act at her best; that she will be courageous, honest, cooperative, and helpful; that she will be unselfish and even sacrificial; that she will not give up when the going is hard, and will get back on her feet when she is knocked down; that she will be happy to give what she can both to individuals and to the community.

No young person, no adult, can wholly live up to these expectations without being a paragon. But the home and the community that expect a great deal from their members will tend to get a great deal; and the home and community that expect little or nothing in the way of response will get nothing, or little—*from the very same people!*

Expectation does not need to be expressed in words. People outside your particular community can feel it in your manner.

A group of fourteen-year-old boys are on school property, looking vaguely for trouble.

"Will you boys please leave the campus. You're not supposed to be here."

If you stand there and wait to see if they leave, you'll wait a long time, and will be called a few choice epithets. If you turn your back immediately and go into your office, they'll delay a few minutes to prove their independence, and then ten to one they'll leave. The crisp "please" makes them feel *they* have helped make the decision; it hasn't been entirely yours. Turning your back indicates your expectation that of course they will leave. And almost always they do.

Act as if you expected to be obeyed and even strangers will tend to obey you. During the war, I permitted the girls to have their junior prom in a hotel that was managed by a patron of the school. My wife and I were going down the stairs to the ballroom with a group of our students and their dates behind us. The bar was at the foot of the stairs on our right, and I heard a boy behind me say, "Let's stop and have a drink."

Without looking around I said very firmly, "Nobody's having a drink tonight." I was angry that the boy had even suggested it.

I heard whispering behind me, followed by a very respectful "Could you tell me, sir, why we can't have a drink?"

I turned around abruptly, prepared to tell him exactly why, and found myself face to face with a sailor and his girl, who were unconnected with the school.

"I'm very sorry," I said. "I thought you were part of my group. Go ahead and have anything you want."

My own students, who had been trying to keep straight faces to see how far the situation would go, burst into laughter.

The young man was relieved. "Gee, sir," he said, "I saw all these people drinking at the tables and didn't understand why you said we couldn't. Thanks a lot," he added, as if I had still given him permission! Expect the best, even the unusual, from young people, and you will tend to get it. And of course they are going to expect something unusual from you. It's a two-way street.

3 The Expectation of Courage: Outward Crisis

Paula

In some way that I cannot wholly explain, the need for certain kinds of people in a community tends to produce them. These persons in turn create in the community the qualities that make it unique.

The community can be a home as well as a school, even though most of my illustrations are from the school which my wife and I headed for many years.

At this school we have always expected the heroic. There was no other way that a school which was starting with six boarders and twenty-seven day students could survive, let alone flourish. We needed heroic teachers who would teach for practically no salary at first. We needed students heroic enough to come to so tiny an institution: three old buildings on an acre of land. We needed faith and sacrifice and valor, but we needed them just as much years later when the school had well over 300 girls and fourteen buildings. It just wasn't quite as obvious, and that is one of the failures of our education.

The need for valor never dies: the battle against odds, the integrity that will not be shaken, the courage to move forward when the slow, seductive voices of retreat are blowing in the wind.

We have not recognized the generation gap. We have not been afraid to love young people, and most of them have not been afraid to love us in return. They say it in their own way, not necessarily in ours. We have been willing to talk to them about anything in the world—including ourselves.

And they came.

Of the eighteen new boarders in the third year of our stay here, ten girls shaped the school for years to come, along with two of the new day pupils. The law of averages wasn't working here. The school needed these girls at a critical time in its history, and the girls rose to the school's need for them. One of them was named Paula.

She was an attractive girl, with a very pleasant, relaxed personality. Her home background was obviously warm and close. From the eighth grade to the end of her sophomore year, she was a happy-go-lucky rule breaker, although she took her punishments good-naturedly and obviously enjoyed the school.

At the beginning of her junior year, I called her in.

"Paula," I asked her, "do you like it here?"

She looked at me with surprise, and smiled.

"Oh, sir, you know I love this school."

"Well, then, don't you think you've raised the devil enough? Don't you think it's time you settled down and started to think what you could do for the school, and some of the things you might stand for?"

She was immediately sober.

"I think you're right, sir," she said, "I guess it's time I grew up. I'll try."

"Good—and thank you."

That year she became a leader in the school, and the next year she was made a student officer.

It was that year that the nightmare of every head-master happened, for the first and only time. A man broke into the girls' dormitory at 1:00 A.M.

He made one fatal mistake. He went up to the third floor room where Paula was sleeping with her two room-mates. Paula woke up and saw him in the room.

While the man went through the dresser drawers of the three girls, she slipped her bare leg under the cover and waited until he had finished. He came over to her bed, but she didn't move. She heard him tiptoe out of the room. He opened the door of the infirmary, saw that no one was there, and started quietly down the stairs. We learned later that he had already been in the other two rooms occupied by students on the third floor. He did not go into the nurse's room.

When Paula heard him going down the carpeted stairs, she carefully woke her two roommates and explained the situation. A quiet conference and then all three girls crept to the top of the stairs and at a whispered one, two, three screamed at the top of their voices.

Have you ever heard three healthy sixteen-year-olds scream in the dead of night in a dormitory where everyone was sound asleep? The intruder never had. He ran down the stairs at breakneck speed and the girls heard the heavy front door slam shut. The Dean rushed out into the hall as the three girls from the top floor ran down to tell her what had happened. She called the police and then called me in the next house. I rushed into pants, shirt, and shoes and ran over to Main House at full speed.

Just as I turned into the front porch, a man stepped from behind a pillar and with a look, I suspect, of great satisfaction grabbed me by the shoulders and said, "Where do you think *you're* going?" It was a policeman. Obviously, at 1:30 A.M. I did not look like a headmaster running to the rescue.

"Let me go," I said, "I'm the headmaster. There's been a man in this house, and I want to see whether the girls are all right."

"What's your name?" he asked suspiciously.

"I'm Ralph Rutenber. I'm the headmaster. These girls are in my charge. I have the key to this house, and you can watch me open the door, but *I'm going in*! Stay right behind me, if you want to."

I put the key in the lock, and he came in with me, staying near the door. I moved into the large hallway. The girls were all sitting on the stairs, with Paula and the Dean in the center. Some were crying, one girl was sobbing, "I want to go home." But Paula and her two roommates were as composed as if screaming burglars away were a nightly event. I was relieved to find that no one had been harmed, but I thought to myself, "This is the end of the school. Every girl will call up her parents now or in the morning, and they'll all be withdrawn tomorrow."

The nurse was talking. "There were two squirrels in my room this afternoon because you girls won't use your screens," she said. "When I heard the girls scream, I thought the squirrels had come back. I rushed over to the three girls and said: 'Where are they? Where are they?' Paula said: 'They! There was only one!' 'There were two here this afternoon,' I said. 'Didn't you see them?'"

The nurse finished her story: "You should have seen the girls' faces when I said there were two of them, and then you should have seen my face when I understood they were talking about a man and not a couple of squirrels!"

Paula, Carol, and Marian—the three roommates—led the laughter, and I sensed that the tension was breaking.

"You haven't heard anything yet," I said. "When I

ran over from Downing after the Dean phoned, the policeman at the door grabbed me and growled, 'Where do you
think *you're* going?' "

There was a shout of laughter. The policeman who
had been searching the grounds looked puzzled as he came
through the front door to report that the intruder could
not be found.

"Thank you," I said. "You have all the information.
Why don't you go ahead and continue your investigation?"

I turned to the twenty-two girls on the staircase and
landing. "I'll stay here all night, so you needn't be worried.
My wife is visiting her mother, as you know. I'll go up into
the infirmary as soon as I can get my pajamas."

The girls were amused. "Sir, who's going to chaperone
you?" one of them asked, and everyone laughed.

They went to bed and I stayed in the infirmary. I was
downstairs well before breakfast in the morning to spread
the news myself before the students broke it.

A girl named Joan happened to be "on duty" that
morning. As she came in from the lower dormitory, Howard
Hall, I told her that a man had broken into Main House last
night.

"A man!" she said, with apparent consternation. "A
man!" she repeated, as if scared to death. "Just my luck!
The first time a man is in one of the dormitories at night,
he has to pick Main House instead of Howard Hall."

As the girls sat down to breakfast, I told of what had
happened, including the nurse's story of the two squirrels;
Paula's comment that when she first looked up from her
bed and saw a man in her room she thought it must be I;
my own "arrest"; and finally Joan's comment that morning. The room rocked with laughter. I never got so much
as a phone call from any parent, although later one of
them, Paula's father, said he hoped I hadn't been too up-

set. The unbelievable young and the equally incredible parents!

At a time of crisis, give me teenagers.

You can read all the books about crisis in the classroom, crisis in the home, crisis in society, and no doubt crisis among the angels, and you will gain much insight. But if you live on a day-to-day basis with young people, you will revise your definitions of education and crisis to a point where they will be unrecognizable amidst the jargon of the experts.

You will throw out the gimmicks first: the panaceas that never pan out; the innovations that die in the pages of a bestseller or between the beginning and end of a brilliant speech to a captive group of tired teachers; and the technical gadgets that end up in the dust of the second floor closet.

You will redefine "crisis" as a time in a person's life when significant change takes place. The time may be a moment; it may be four years. There are likely to be many crises while students learn, along with their teachers and counselors, the important and difficult lessons of life: that there is no such thing as a frustration-free existence; that defeat may be what happens to you but victory is what you are; that acts—and words—have consequences; that hatred, to use Fromm's great phrase, "is unlived life"; that success is measured not by money but by meaning; that response to the needs of others is the answer to our own deepest needs; and that, in the words of Thornton Wilder, "there is a land of the living and a land of the dead, and the bridge is love, the only survival, the only meaning. . . ."

Crises? They appear whenever a girl is face to face with a fact that will not let her go, or an obligation that she does not wish to accept, or a temptation that whispers, why not?

Crises? They face the teachers as well as the taught.

How shall I motivate the child who does not seem to want to learn? How shall I gain her confidence and trust when she appears so resentful, hostile, and suspicious—even of my motives? How shall I find out what has made her angry, or afraid? How shall I handle this disciplinary situation so that neither the child nor the community will be damaged, and so that each may learn something of value? How shall I love her when she seems to hate me or my class? And how shall I help her—if I don't?

At MacDuffie, concepts are only the attire of people. The imperatives of society are cries to us from other persons we know—and don't know. The identity crisis is not a concept of Erik Erikson's, but one's daughter trying to develop confidence in spite of her fears of failure; serenity in the face of a world with the jitters; ethical and religious ideals in a moment of history when other voices, in other rooms, are extolling the "roses and raptures" of the drugs that blow the mind, and the acts that close the heart.

The outer crises of education are only important because, in solving them, we are able to continue to deal with the inner crises of mind and character that are the continuing stuff of education.

A man creeping into a dormitory late at night is a crisis. But the kind of parents I had knew that the real crisis was the reaction of the girls. The parents of the three girls who screamed the intruder away must have known that their daughters possibly averted a tragedy that could have scarred a girl for life. The girls knew with what humor-clad courage they had been saved. They were wise enough to realize that they had seen and heard on the staircase at Main House and the breakfast table the next morning something more unforgettable than the danger that walked at midnight. I'm sure if they had begged their parents to take them out of MacDuffie they would have been withdrawn. But they didn't. And I was too young a head-

master to know until after the event that out of such incidents great communities, undergirded by courage and
sacrifice and affection, are born.

Naturally we do not want to develop or reveal courage
by any such hazard as the one just described. We do not
open our doors to robbers; nor invite pushers on the campus to test the emotional stability of our students; nor con-
trive a flood or fire or any near tragedy to bring out the
heroic in our students. We quite properly install new locks
and hire night watchmen. We take every precaution to
avoid physical crisis, and we should.

However, we are also scared to death that our children
will have to face those inward crises that can give them
ego-strength. We do not want them to be heroic; we want
them to be comfortable. We do not ask them to give; we
beg them to receive. We are afraid to drop the second
shoe.

A final word about Paula. Late one afternoon her
mother called and told me that Paula's brother had been
killed in the war; that she wanted me to tell Paula; and
that she and her husband would be up right after dinner
to take her home. I knew that Paula adored her big
brother.

I called her into the office.

"Little one," I said, "your mother called me this afternoon about your brother. I'm afraid I have very bad news
for you."

She knew at once. I saw the tears come to her eyes,
but her voice was steady.

"Has he been killed?"

"Yes, dear, he has. I'm so sorry."

I put my arms around her and she wept quietly.

"May I go to my room, sir?"

"By all means. Shall I tell the other girls?"

"I'll tell them."

"I'll be up to see you just before dinner."

As the first bell for dinner rang, I went upstairs. Girls were coming out of her room, crying. Several of her closest friends remained.

"Paula," I said, "there's no reason why you should go down to dinner. I can have your roommates bring it up to you. They can bring their own meals too and stay with you till your parents come."

Paula said nothing for a few moments.

"Sir," she said, "could all of you please leave me to myself for a few minutes? Then I can decide what I want to do, if you don't mind."

We left the room and went downstairs to the dining room. Girls were weeping quietly at the tables. Others were ostentatiously busy getting bread, putting food on the tables, talking as normally as they could.

In a few minutes Paula walked into the dining room. Her head was high as she took her place and apologized for being late. The girls looked up in amazement and the whole room became silent. Then a girl got up to refill a pitcher of milk. It was a roommate of Paula's. The tension dissolved and the meal went on in the usual way. When I rang the bell, Paula's parents were outside in the hall, and she ran toward them sobbing.

4 The Expectation of Courage: Inner Crisis

How do you produce a girl like Paula?

How did she find as roommates two girls who would be as courageous as she was? How did those three girls with the help of the Dean and the nurse calm the rest of the girls in the dormitory and develop a spirit of comradeship with one another and concern for the school that in many instances was wholly out of character with their usual responses? And why did whatever humor Joan and I were able to find in the situation and express in the dormitory and dining room give the final blast of laughter to the already crumbling edifice of fear?

And what did the parents sense in their children or in the school that kept them from dialing the headmaster next day and expressing their abrupt indignation that such a thing could happen; their fear for the future safety of their children; or their decision to take the child out at once? And if the child did remain, just what were we planning to do that would guarantee to the concerned parents that an incident like this could not happen again?

We had answers ready for all these questions, but we were never asked.

I said in the last chapter that the inner crises of mind and character were the stuff of education in both home and school. Although the examples in Chapter 3 of outer crises were dramatic in one case and tragic in another, an intruder in the dormitory and a brother killed in the war, each outward crisis carried its own inner crisis, as in the tragedies of Shakespeare. The outward crisis may or may not be dramatic in itself; but the drama of the inner crisis is inescapable.

If crisis represents a moment of decision, a turning point for better or worse, an emotionally significant event or radical change in a person's life, a crucial state of affairs—to use the most common dictionary definitions—then crisis is the trigger-finger of decision, of emotionally significant events that activate or change people. If this is true, then education should seize upon those events which may discharge into decisions or turning points in a young person's way of thinking or acting, and try to commute them into the centrality that we call character. This is the invisible curriculum of every home and school.

Mary

When Mary came to the school, she knew she was going to study a curriculum consisting of English, algebra, languages, science, the arts, and history. She did not know that there was an invisible curriculum also awaiting her, in which she would be expected to contribute to the school a kind of courage and unselfishness she had not shown before.

She was tall for a ninth grader, very young and awkward, with two much older sisters. She had been most excited during her visit the spring before. She talked almost like an adult. Her parents looked at her proudly while I interviewed her, as if to say, "Look at this wonderful creature we have brought you." And indeed she was impressive, although obviously self-willed.

On the opening day of school, I noticed that her parents stayed with her right up to six o'clock, although they had arrived just after lunch. I noticed at dinner that she looked weepy, but so did other new girls. We are used to homesickness. It usually disappears after about three weeks.

In less than three days, there is a knock at my door.

"Sir, may I see you?" It is Mary.

"Sure, come on in."

She doesn't beat about the bush. "I want to go home." She is aggressive because she is afraid I'll say no. She is holding back the tears. Homesickness is no fun; it is a real though temporary sickness of the spirit and is not subject to rational analysis. The worst thing to do is to lecture her about her obligations. Suggest, but don't condemn. She has got to lecture herself, if you're going to win this one.

"Do your parents want you to come home?"

"My father said I could, if I were too unhappy." (Father disregarded my suggestion to say just the opposite. I'll call him again later.)

"Did he say he wanted you to come?"

"He said I could—if I wanted to."

"I know he said you could. But do you think he wants you to?"

"He wants me to be happy," she snaps, on the defensive. "I'll never be happy in this place." The tone is disagreeable and scornful. The place is obviously the Black Hole of Calcutta, where she has been whipped, starved, and put into solitary. Not your beloved, wonderful school. She seems very unattractive, as people do when they are criticizing something very close to you. You'd like to tell her to pack up her bag and call her parents. But of course you don't. You're a teacher and this is your student. You have obligations to keep your students and to win over the supposedly unwinsome.

"How about your mother? Does she want you to stay?"

She is near tears again.

"They both want me to be happy."

"That's not what I'm asking. Do they want you to come home?"

"I just don't like it here."

"I know that." (I don't remind her that she has been here only three days.) "But you haven't answered my question. Do they want you to come home?"

"They don't want me to—but I can come home if I want to. And I hate this place! You can't keep me here."

She is sobbing, and I hand her a Kleenex. You can't run a girls' school without Kleenex. I wait until she is calmer.

"Mary, let me talk for a while. I know I've given you a hard time, but let me say once and for all: I can't possibly keep you here. I know that. We don't have any high walls, or doors that lock from the inside. The night watchman won't be here till six. You can walk off the grounds at any time you really want to, and get a bus or a train and head for home. I'm not going to watch you. Any girl can do it. And as far as your parents go, they won't send you back against your will. You've won the battle. They're completely licked. You can clobber them on the head the minute you're on the telephone and tell them to come and get you. They can't stand knowing you're unhappy. They'll come.

"But they don't want you to leave, and you know it. I'm hoping you'll stay. I'm betting on it. I think you love them enough to do what *they* want. I know how much you want to go. I'm asking you to do a hard thing—probably the hardest thing you've ever done.

"They've invested something besides money in Mac-

Duffie. They've invested their hopes. This is the school you wanted to come to, and the one they liked the best, too.

"You don't owe me anything. I won't lose my job if you leave, although I won't feel happy to see you go. I just hope you'll do the hard thing—and stay. I'm hoping you'll make your parents happy this time, no matter how unhappy you feel about the school. Think it over, will you? And come in and see me tomorrow at this same time. OK?"

She walks out slowly. So many new ideas to think about: she has won the battle; she has gotten what she wants; she doesn't have to stay—but she has been asked to stay to make her parents happy! What about *her* happiness?

If the parents hold firm, the chances are ten to one that she will stay for that year. But the father has promised to take her home if she requests it. I have a long talk with him on the phone, but he feels he should keep his promise. I cannot tell him not to; I believe in keeping promises, too. The mother is angry with the father for promising. It is going to be up to Mary.

I get a call from the parents that night that Mary wants to come home, and they will be down to get her at noon the next day. I am sure I have lost but decide to make one more try. I used to be able to say that the parents were legally bound to pay the full year's tuition for a day or a week's stay, and it often changed the decision of the girl, after she had made the usual wild promises to earn the money herself during the summer. But now insurance takes care of most of the money, and Mr. Stone had taken out the insurance. And Mary knew it.

I called Mary in the next morning.

"I understand your parents are on their way to pick you up."

"Yes, sir, that's right." She sounded very respectful this morning. It was as if she were almost sorry that she had gotten her way.

"You told them to come, I assume."

"Yes, sir."

"The reason I asked you that is because once in a great while the parents are so homesick they hope the girl will tell them to come—and they come before she can change her mind. But I don't think that's true in this case. Your father is living up to his promise, although I think he's sorry he made it. What do you think?"

"I think maybe so."

"Are you all packed?"

"Yes, sir, I packed last night after lights."

I knew the girls all pitched in. There is a certain excitement when a girl goes home—even when she is expelled. It is a happening. If the girl is going of her own volition, she is something of a hero. She has refused to stay. She has gotten her way. The new girls who are homesick will be even more so now. They will call up their parents and tell them "Everyone is leaving!"

I turned to Mary for one last try. I spoke briskly, in a matter-of-fact voice, almost a commanding one.

"Mary, when they come, I want you to give them the surprise of their lives. I want you to tell them to go back home. I want you to tell them you have decided to stay, in spite of your unhappiness in the school. I want you to do what you know you ought to, and I make you one promise, which I shall keep. If at the end of the year, you don't want to return to MacDuffie, I'll fight on your side. I'll tell your parents you gave it a fair try. I'll tell them not to make you return against your will. Now, run along."

I went back to my office for the usual hectic day. I went to lunch but didn't see Mary. There was no sign of her parents nor of a car with a New York license. At quarter of six, I left the office to pick up my wife for dinner. Mary was waiting outside.

"I sent them home," she said. Her lips were trembling,

and she had obviously been crying. I put my arm around her.

"Mary," I said, "I think you're terrific. I think you're wonderful. I'm proud to know you. Thanks a lot."

Mary was not yet thirteen when this incident occurred —the youngest girl in her class. She had done more than conquer her homesickness; she had given something to the adult world. For once she was the fairy godmother, not Cinderella in the kitchen waiting for the adult world to supply her with glass slippers and a prince.

For once she was an adult in the seat of power, like the centurion in the New Testament: "I say to this man, go, and he goeth; and to another, come, and he cometh." I would not have given her the power to make that particular decision, had I been her parents; but she had it, and I wanted to teach her the responsibility to *others* that goes with power. Above all, I wanted her to learn the excitement of giving, even of sacrifice, in a life which I gathered had been one of relentless receiving. The permissive and indulgent parent is being indulgent and permissive primarily to himself. He is hogging the "give" in the family, leaving his child only the undernourishing crumbs of "take."

I said "Thanks a lot" to Mary, and there will be some who think that the phrase is merely a sprig of courtesy, a touch of green in the gray boughs of the everyday, a harmless and pleasant convention, mostly between adults.

On the contrary, "Thank you" is one of the most potent phrases in the language for bridging the generation gap.

"Thank you" and "would you mind" are equalizing terms. If I say to the caretaker of the school, "John, would you mind putting sand on the ice in front of Howard Hall," I am giving him a command in the form of a suggestion. He is intelligent. He knows he is to put sand in the slippery place. But he also knows I have worded the order in a way that implies an expectation of agreement on his part, as well as of performance. He is open to suggest to me that perhaps he should put the sand first in front of the class-room building. It is a discussion between equals: two men who don't want a teacher or student to fall on the ice. The equalization is felt by both men genuinely; otherwise, the method of wording would be manipulative. The fact that one man has the power to enforce his suggestion is ir-relevant. That power is too far in the background to be part of the situation. We are all employees of each other. "Thank you" is a completion, not just a courtesy. It says, in effect, "I appreciate the way we can work together and the kind of person you are."

"Thank you" to children and young people tells them a great many things. It tells them that they are part of the adult world, participate in its courtesies, are appreciated for their work or attitude, and are treated as citizens. There is a disdain for young people on the part of many adults which does not so much criticize them as ignore them. It goes back to the Puritan idea that duties, espe-cially those incumbent on the young, should produce no gratitude because they *are* duties, things that ought to be done anyway. The male chauvinists who growl that men shouldn't be grateful for the domestic and child-rearing labors of their wives because that's what they're supposed to do are of the same ilk. And of course there are female chauvinists, too.

So, I thanked Mary for telling her parents to go home. No doubt she should have done it anyway, but the fact that we ought to do certain things doesn't make it any easier to do them. I wasn't about to analyze her past life or any possible failures in her upbringing. The situation was now; the decision was now. It was the beginning of her growing up. It was a great help to me and a great contribution to the kind of school I wanted to have. Why shouldn't I thank her?

I am well aware it can be argued that all these examples prove is that four girls showed courage; that the courage was not necessarily due to the expectations of the community; that maybe the courage was in their genes, or maybe their glands were connected with their guts.

Maybe.

I don't pretend to be able to unravel the strands of human motives or human actions. However, we do know, whether we are behaviorists or analysts, that human beings do not operate in a vacuum but in an environment, both external and internal, physical, mental, emotional, and moral. That environment is both the world of other people, constrained by time and space and organization, and also the mysterious inner world of core and essence.

Our job is neither metaphysics nor biology. The teacher and the parent must in word and attitude expect such reactions as courage, cooperation, and thoughtfulness toward others in situations where the opposite qualities could easily be displayed. We must be consciously alert for those situations, even though obviously we cannot anticipate the more dramatic ones. Above all, we must express to the young person our appreciation for her contribution to the community.

5 Overexpectation and the Para-communities

So far we have been talking about community expectation met successfully by the individual. But no book on young people, or any other group, is a continuous success story. Obviously, our children (whether of school or home) do not always live up to our expectations—nor do we to theirs. The home and the school are competing with counter communities, communities which are essentially in opposition to the kind of character that we are trying to produce.

The counter communities are stridently against us —against not only our goals but the methods we use to obtain them. It's not hard to identify the Drug Culture; the Navel Gazers ("I've got to find myself first"); and the golden improbabilities of the New Morality. At least they are out in the open, and we know that the battle is joined.

More difficult to combat are the para-communities, which I define as the communities that, quite honestly, believe in the same goals for young people as we do, but pursue these ends with means so misconceived and flawed that the ends themselves are altered and twisted out of shape and often indistinguishable from those of the counter communities. Indeed, it would be fair to say that the means employed, often innocently, in the para-communities drive the young person into the counter communities from which his counselors would save him.

When we look carefully at these para-communities, we find that they are the same old stand-bys of the ages, the true communities of home and school that have lost their way in the battle for the minds and souls (let's not be afraid of that word) of young people. They are the Sunday Service of our virtues; the orotund syllables and frilled sleeves of the Bishop; the Altar of our Ideals, misted in incense and glowing with candlelight. They are What We Believe In but cannot effect in the dirty-gray world of Monday morning.

The communities of home and school that have lost their way. . . .

On Parents

To some, parents are the comedy of our culture—a comedy that is laced with the bitterness of the young, the jeers of the intellectual, and the belly laughs of the Bunker set. The stereotypes move among the angels (we are the angels, of course: our children are grown up or not yet born), going through their sad routines like living things. Not for parents, say their critics, is the stark kingdom of sex, the naked battle of the plunger, the agonized and exquisite hunger to be filled. That is the prerogative of young people, as they fumble with buttons in a locked room in a college dormitory, inquire about the pill, and wonder what the partner really thinks of them. College presidents are the only people in our society who can maintain without penalty quarters for the cohabitation of the young at any hour of the day or night. Of course, one former college president, Mary Bunting of Radcliffe, told a reporter as quoted in *Time* that the girls at Radcliffe were so busy with their homework that they didn't have time for sexual intercourse.

Whether there was a surge of applications for Radcliffe after this remark or whether the number dropped off has not been recorded.

The jokes about parents are bandied about in the halls of academe especially. "We shouldn't have had any children until we had had three"; "parents are the last people who ought to have children"; and, to quote from a speech given arrogantly on Parents Day when private schools could still be arrogant: "We shall ask you for money, but do not think that you can give enough or withhold enough to have the slightest influence on the way your son will be brought up at _____ (a famous boys' school). We shall take complete charge of bringing him up in the way that we consider best for him."

I have found parents almost uniformly helpful, concerned, and devoted to their offspring. However, they have been brainwashed by every owl-eyed expert who has figured out a new caveat. They have been exhorted, scolded, viewed with amazement, and departed from in sorrow. If their children behave well, they have been repressive; if they behave badly, the home is permissive.

If the home has lost its way and become a para-community rather than a true one, it is because the experts have urged the parents to build up their children's confidence and ego-strength—and I am all for it—but have forgotten to help the parents build up their own. Only the strong parent can make the child strong; only the parent who is sure of his own values and methods can produce the young person who is confident of his.

The overexpectation of parents for their children is a mixture of fear, pride—and the wrong kind of expectations; that is, values. Fear predominates.

The fear of being a bad parent is far greater in my

own counseling experience than that of being a bad husband or wife. After all, husband and wife are of the same generation; they feel at home with each other; to some extent, certainly, they speak the same language. If they have a fight, there is no particular challenge involved, no feeling that they have "lost caste" with their mate and have shown themselves up as somehow "inferior" because of a disagreement.

Archie Bunker is still the all-American husband, except to the sophisticated and the compassionate. His argumentative manner, the thoroughly disagreeable looks and words directed to his wife are in the merry vein of the old grouch with a heart—if you can find it—of gold. They are all out of step but him, and Edith humors him and loves him as her Big Baby Boy. The audience loves it.

But let "little goil" tell him off, and the Big Bear has all his defenses down and is not ashamed to show that he has been hurt by her insensitivity to him, and her lack of love and appreciation. There is a touch of guilt and even of pleading that she be sweet to her dear old father, while he can tell his wife with a snarl to "shut up." He can't bear to fail as a father, but as a husband, it is all Edith's fault if she makes him mad. He was never harangued by a group of intellectuals to be a kind and thoughtful husband. He has grown up in the Age of the Child.

In the para-communities of home, the parents love their children just as much as in the true communities. But their fear of making mistakes, plus their pride in "prestige" achievements, cause them to value performance that can be measured to their satisfaction (and conversation) rather than the personal qualities that will eventually bring out whatever potential the student may have.

"It Was the *Best* Butter"
(*Alice in Wonderland*)

"What worries me," I said to her parents, "is the intensity of her desire to get into Smithcliff. We send a lot of girls to other colleges, and many of them prefer a coed college. But she seems to feel that it will be a family disgrace if she doesn't get into Smithcliff. Somehow or other she has gotten that idea."

"We haven't knowingly given it to her," said her mother. "I think there is no doubt that we have assumed that she would make Smithcliff. We knew that she was doing C+ work at MacDuffie, and we know that she is an alumna daughter. Don't you think she will get in?"

You can say almost anything to parents as long as they know you love their child. I decided to say it. "You know, Mrs. Bowdoin, you are really showing me one reason why Karen is so obsessed with Smithcliff. I have told you that I am worried about the intensity of her ambition, that she seems to feel she will be a disgrace to her family, and of course to herself, if she isn't accepted. And you tell me that you haven't knowingly pressured her. You say why you think she can make it—and then ask me in surprise if I don't think she will 'get in'."

She looked upset. "You're telling me that my attitude is a form of pressure."

"What do *you* think?"

"I think you're right. We shall certainly tell her that we don't care whether or not she makes Smithcliff."

"May I put it a little more strongly? You cannot merely tell her that. She won't accept it, no matter how often you tell her it's true. You have to believe it yourself. You have to believe it with all your heart. You have to say to yourself—and mean it: 'This is my daughter. I love her very much. She is a wonderful person, and she is mine. I couldn't care less whether she goes to Smithcliff, or a community college, or Podunk U. I want her to have a college education, because she is capable of it, and I feel that it will enrich her experience. But where she gets it is not impor-

could do the work at Smithcliff if accepted. But that doesn't mean they'll be accepted. And what of it? Do you want a college education or do you just want Smithcliff?"

She sounds hopeless. "You don't think I'll make it, do you? I know my Boards weren't high. My parents will be so disappointed."

My parents.

Make it ... get in. The four words that headmasters hate the most. My work is cut out for me. Karen is a fine girl, and a solid, though not outstanding, student. I want to make her feel good about herself and her abilities; but I must also prepare her for the realistic probability that she will not be accepted at Smithcliff. Even if she "makes it" we have a job to do. She is *equating her worth as a person with getting into a particular college.* No matter how unimportant the ambition may seem to us as adults, as educators we know that nothing is more important than a person's sense of worth. I need help from Karen's parents.

Mr. and Mrs. Bowdoin were attractive, intelligent, and cordial. They had no idea they were putting pressure on Karen. They knew that Karen did good work; they knew I would recommend her for character and contribution (hers, not her father's); and they had understood that alumnae daughters were given some special consideration. They had assumed that she would "make" Smithcliff. Second and third choices had been rather casually discussed. These people were not professional college counselors. They were not attending MacDuffie.

But Karen was. And she knew that she got her results from hard work and long hours. She knew that there were many girls in her class who learned faster, remembered better, and expressed themselves with ease and confidence. She always felt she was climbing up a slippery rock, clutching, clutching, for Smithcliff. And she might slip down and land in Podunk U. The young can be snobbish too.

For "butter" substitute "college"!

"Sir, may I see you?"

"Sure, come on in. What's the trouble?"

"Sir, do you think I'm going to make Smithcliff?" She is tense. The middle finger of her right hand is rubbing against the arm of her chair.

"It's a good college. There are a lot of others equally good, and maybe better for you. What is so wonderful about Smithcliff?" (I know what is so wonderful. It is unattainable.)

"Well, sir, my mother went to Smithcliff. My aunt went to Smithcliff. Almost all my relatives went to Smithcliff." (I'd love to tell her where I wish all her relatives had gone!)

"You know, little one, you're not your mother, or your aunt, or your relatives. You're yourself. Let's leave them out of the picture and concentrate on you."

"I can't seem to get them out of the picture. Will you recommend me?"

"Yes, I'll recommend you. But that doesn't mean you'll be accepted."

Her face brightens. She has scored what she thinks is a big point.

"I'm sure I'll be accepted if you recommend me. In fact, the Director of Admissions said so!"

"Now, wait a minute. I want you to think very hard. The Director of Admissions didn't say that. What she said was that my recommendation would be a very important part of your credentials. She may even have said that it would be the most important part. I've been a headmaster for quite a while; I would hope my recommendations would carry weight. But that doesn't mean that if I recommend you, you're automatically accepted at one of the most competitive colleges in the country. I'll recommend any girl in this school to any college where I think she can do the work. No doubt more than half my seniors

tant to me. It is not a part of our relationship as mother and daughter, father and daughter.' "

Both parents are listening intently.

"Look," I said, "I know you love Karen and she loves you. And she knows you love her; no adolescent can be fooled about that. However, no adolescent sits down and calmly reasons out her problems. Karen is not about to say to herself: 'Of course, my parents love me, and they will love me just as much whether I make Smithcliff or not. After all, what I want is a college education, and I can get that in many good colleges.'

"You must realize that Smithcliff means something to her, as it might not to somebody else. If her unconscious mind spoke, it would say something like this: 'I'm not sure I'm as smart as the really smart girls in this school, but if I make this college, everybody will think so—and I will, too. I haven't been a leader at MacDuffie. I didn't make the hockey team, and I was sure I'd get into the Glee Club, but I didn't. Sometimes I just feel as if I were no good for anything. I *must* get into Smithcliff. I want my father to think I'm just as smart as my mother. And of course my brother is at Princeton. I just can't face anybody if I don't make it. I'll just go off to join the Peace Corps in Africa, or get a job somewhere.'

"She wants to show you that she's really successful in one field. She wants to hand you Smithcliff on a platter, like the head of John the Baptist. 'Look how much I love you. I've given you Smithcliff. How much you must love me for doing it. You can boast to your friends that I have made Smithcliff. I don't care how many people you tell. Daddy, you didn't think I could do it, did you? Aren't you proud of me? I made the same college that mother did. You love me, don't you? You do love me, don't you?' "

My voice had become as tense as Karen's when she is talking to the college counselor. Mr. Bowdoin was the first to speak.

"Dr. Rutenber," he said, "you are worried about the

effect of failure on Karen, and so am I, after hearing you talk. You almost sound as if you think she is disturbed."

"I don't think Karen is disturbed in any psychiatric sense. But I believe that this is a bad time for her to fail in her own opinion, even though not in ours. She has worked very hard at MacDuffie to get the grades she has gotten. She is intelligent, of course, but she is not what we call academic, or scholastic. What the S.A.T.'s are testing or trying to test is what I like to call 'book ability,' the ability to learn with varying degrees of success from books. It is not the most important ability in the world by a long shot, but it is the kind a girl needs if she is going to Smithcliff. Karen lacks the quick, conceptual grasp of the superior student. What of it? She has staying power, which is the more important quality. But it isn't important to her at the moment."

"What shall we do?" asked Mrs. Bowdoin. "I'm very upset, and I want to do everything I can to help her. I don't know why I didn't recognize all this sooner."

I told them not to punish themselves, that this was her junior year and we all had time to work on the problem. The problem was to change her values. In the process, their own values would change, as mine have changed by working with young people.

What is important?—that is the real question. A minor writer, Christopher Morley, said a very major thing a long time ago:

"If we discovered that we had only five minutes left to say all we wanted to say, every telephone booth would be occupied by people calling other people to stammer that they loved them."

Not that they were proud of their success in making Smithcliff, or becoming president of their firm, or winning the 100-yard dash, or making money, or belonging to the best clubs, or knowing the most prominent people. Not with only five minutes left.

6 Listening with the Third Ear: The Hidden Motive

The overexpectation doesn't have to be academic, although this is the type that we deal with the most in schools. But there are many other kinds of expectation that the student just cannot meet. Sometimes the parental assumption is voiced; sometimes unvoiced but very apparent. Sometimes the overexpectation is so covered up, perhaps even from the parent, that it takes a Third Ear to discover it.

To listen with the Third Ear—the phrase is Theodore Reik's—is to listen for the real meaning behind a person's words. It is an attempt to hear, not what a person thinks he is saying, but what he is really trying to tell you. Listening with the Third Ear can be called a technique because it is conscious: it is a way of evaluating the real and often hidden meaning. But the evaluation is more than analytic and intellectual, a learned response to a given set of words and ideas. It is also intuitive and sympathetic, representing one life experience reacting with understanding and compassion to another through words that cannot or will not convey the real substance of what is felt—and often defended against a reality too bitter to accept.

Nancy

"Sir, may I see you?"

"Sure, come in."

Nancy was a new girl, an outstanding student, somewhat plump, with a face roughened by acne. Her mother was a caterer, her father an engineer.

"Sir, I want to talk to you about religion."

"That's fine, unless you think your parents might object. What *is* your religious background?"

"I'm a Catholic, but I don't believe in God at all. I know you must, from your chapel talks. Can you tell me why anyone should believe in God?"

I explained to her that, as she well knew, people defined God differently; that not even the philosophers could prove the existence of God unless you granted them certain assumptions; that I thought it was more reasonable to believe in God than not to believe in Him; and that I would be glad to give her my own reasons for believing in a Supreme Person not myself.

It was a good discussion. She obviously enjoyed arguing with me.

"Thank you very much," she said at the end, "you have given me a lot to think about." She smiled and left.

I felt the glow of having done a Good Deed.

The next day, late in the afternoon, she was back in my office.

"Sir, I'm sorry to bother you, but would you mind going over those reasons again. I just seem to be losing my faith entirely."

"Shouldn't you go to your parents, or your priest?" I asked.

"Oh, no," she said. "Mother knows I'm talking to you.

Now, will you give me your reasons again for believing in God?"

I went over them again. She listened brightly, attentively.

"Why don't you comment, now?" I said. "I've talked enough."

She gave me some half-hearted objections. We tossed them back and forth.

"I have to go now," I finally said, "and get ready for dinner."

"Thank you very much, sir," she said, and smiled. "I really understand your reasons now, and I feel much better."

The next morning, my secretary said that Nancy had called from the classroom building. She had seemed upset and would like to see me the fourth period during her study hall.

"Perhaps she's homesick," I thought. But I had a lot of appointments that day and did not see how I could fit her in. I told my secretary to check with her housemother and adviser on possible homesickness, though I had seen no evidence of it myself.

"Tell her I'll see her tomorrow in the fourth period," I said, "but I can't today."

The next day Nancy appeared, but she was no longer smiling.

"I know I'm bothering you," she said, "but I'm so upset. I just seem to be losing all my religious faith. I don't see any real reason for believing in God or any reason for living at all. Why shouldn't I kill myself if I want to?"

She looked unhappy when she said it, but certainly not desperate. Every counselor of young people has heard the threat. We hardly panic, but we do not wholly dismiss it either. There is always that thousandth time,

I gave her the usual reasons why a healthy, highly intelligent girl with a desire to be a lawyer should want to live, the "your-whole-life-before-you" bit, not omitting the contribution she could make to others through her profession. She listened attentively, as always, but not as relaxed as before.

I did not try to make it a discussion.

"Think it over," I said, "and I'm sure you'll agree with me."

She smiled for a brief moment.

"Thank you very much," she said. "I have a lot to think about."

She continued to try to make appointments almost every day, always with a sense of urgency, always with deep apologies for interrupting or taking so much time or making herself such a nuisance—and always coming back to the same questions: "Why believe in God at all? Why live?"

I realized that trotting out my one-two-three-four answers was having no effect whatever. I checked on her carefully without her knowing it. I did not see any other signs of a depression. She seemed happy with her roommate; she was doing very well in her studies. The adjustment to boarding school seemed to be very good. One always says "seemed."

I began to repeat myself on purpose—how many new ways can you say that you believe in God and that life is worth living?—to see whether or not she was really as upset about her loss of faith as she seemed to be. I tried to use exactly the same words I had used the previous day. She listened each time as if she had not heard my arguments before, and thanked me warmly each time for "helping" her. I knew she was much too bright not to know that I was repeating myself regularly. And yet I was convinced that both the urgency to see me and the expressions of gratitude for helping her were genuine.

I was not convinced that she was really as interested in the existence of God or the loss of her religious faith as she wanted to think she was. I was also aware that stu-

dents often like to feel that both they and their problems
are sufficiently important to engage the time and attention of the head of the school; but this did not account for
the almost desperate urgency with which she sought appointments. I did not believe that she was really thinking
of suicide, partly because her manner was so relaxed once
she was in the office and asking me why life was worth
living. I felt there was a missing clue somewhere.

I began to question her about her home, especially
her mother.

"You say your parents know I am talking to you
about religion?"

"Oh, yes. They don't mind."

"Well, that's good. You're the only child, aren't you?"

"Yes, I am, and there are times when I'd like to have
had brothers and sisters."

"Why?"

"I think it would be fun. I also think it would take
some of the heat off me."

"Do you feel your parents put the 'heat' on you? Maybe you're putting it on yourself."

"I don't think I am."

"You're doing very well in your studies. I'm sure your
parents are pleased."

"It's the dances that bug them—especially Mother. I've
told her so many lies. I hope she never shows up at one."

"Why should you tell her lies? Are you pretending to
go to dances and not going?"

I could feel the tension rising in her. Her feet were
crossed at the ankle, and she kept moving her right foot
up and down as if she were keeping time to some unheard
music.

"Oh, I go all right," she said, rather petulantly. "It's
what I tell her afterward that bothers me. But I have to do
it," she added belligerently.

"Have to do what?"

"Look, sir, after every dance my mother calls me up

and asks me how it went. Did the boys ask me to dance? Did they cut in? Was I popular? It's like a baby asking for candy. How can I tell her I'm a wallflower? It would kill her. How can I tell her nobody asked me to dance? How can I tell her I'm fat and have acne, and that boys don't look at me? It's the most important thing in the world to her to believe that I am a belle. So I give her what she wants to hear. Do you understand?"

Her voice had risen sharply, and she was close to tears.

"I tell her the most fantastic stories—and she believes them. I tell her I was the hit of the dance. All the boys wanted to dance with me, but I finally chose the football captain, who was big and handsome. You wouldn't think she'd believe all that stuff, would you, but she does. I can almost see her eyes get big over the phone. She pictures me like a gazelle, floating around the dance floor, delicate and graceful and bewitching—while I sit there by myself, scratching my face and wishing I was dead. Do you hear what I say? Dead, dead—wishing I was dead. No boy ever gave me the time of day or ever will. But I can't tell that to my mother. I think she'd die of shame!"

She was crying. Anger, embarrassment, and frustration were in her sobs. I realized suddenly and sadly why she *had* to see me. I was the date she had never had; I was the male who would listen to her, talk to her, and not reject her—especially if she could find a reason for seeing me which could not fail. And she had found it, whether consciously or unconsciously I did not know.

How could a person in my position refuse to see a girl who was worried about her religious faith? Didn't we have chapel once a week, where I talked about such things? How could a headmaster refuse to talk to a girl who wondered why life was worth living and who might even kill herself, right there in the school? How could he refuse to help anyone who asked for help? Wasn't he talking about concern for others? Well, let him show his concern for me, and listen to me, talk to me, explain to me—never mind how often—anything that will give me a chance to feel that one man, one male, never mind how middle-aged, will make an appointment, at a given time, on a given day, to see me, Me, ME!

"Nancy," I said, "tell your mother the truth and don't worry about her feelings. Adults have to grow up, just like kids. Mothers and fathers have to grow up, just like daughters. I grow up a little every day, I hope. No adult has a right to be treated like a child, and no child has a right to treat an adult as anything but a grown-up person. And don't give a damn whether she's upset or not that the boys aren't swooning over you at every dance. Tell her the truth, and don't be ashamed of it. And don't forget that on every dance floor behind all those plastic smiles at least half the girls are agonizing over whether some lame-brained male is going to find them to his lordship's liking. And what of it?"

I gave her the only kind of advice I could, with the realization that if she were able to follow it, she wouldn't need it. You can sagely tell a shy person that she must forget about herself and think of other people when she is in a group; but if she could forget about herself, she wouldn't be shy.

Many parents do not realize that overexpectation does not necessarily mean nagging. They think that they have not pressured their child because they have not told her constantly that they want her to get high grades or do well on College Boards or "make" a competitive college. But young people are not fooled. Karen knew that her parents "assumed" she would get into Smithcliff, and she was just as tense about the assumption as she would have been if they had screamed their expectation to her once a week. The unvoiced assumption is actually stronger than the nagging admonition, because the latter tends to arouse the kind of explosive anger which is a welcome solvent to obligations, either real or imposed, whereas the child tends to internalize the unvoiced assumptions of the parents regarding his ability to shine in all situations, and thinks it must be his own fault that the effort makes him bleed a little.

This is the trouble with the so-called "common-sense" approach to people's problems, used especially by parents. It assumes that people act reasonably once the reasonable path is pointed out. The orderly mother will say to her disorderly daughter, "Dear, you wouldn't find it so hard to find things if you just had a special place for them, and put them there the moment you are finished with them." What could be more reasonable than this? You take off a dress, and you hang it up instead of dropping it on the floor with your underwear. You take off your sweater and put it in the second drawer, which is for sweaters. Then you know where it is when you want it.

If the daughter could accept this sage advice, her room would be as orderly as her mother's and so would her mind. She wouldn't need the advice in the first place—or she'd need it only once.

But, alas, what is reasonable to mother is extremely painful to daughter. To put each of her articles of clothing in closets and drawers the moment she has taken them off is to checkrein her headlong rush to the showers, to her studies, to the telephone, to her date. Her mind is on the next phase of her life, not on straightening out the physical reminders of her last one. The closet is always there; the drawer will not disengage itself and fly out the window; meanwhile, the floor is broad, friendly, supportive—securely anchored and reassuring. Why waste time doing what can be done later? The fact that "later" never comes does not mean that it won't come this time—later.

And of course more than temperament is often involved. Daughter may have developed a strong sense of guilt that she is not doing the right thing; that she is making work for her mother, as well as herself; that Father may compare her unfavorably to her natural rival. Whatever chances she might have of correcting her tendency to drop everything and get going on something else are usually dissipated by the perfectionism of Mother (orderly people tend to want perfect order, not better order), and by her own uncomfortable sense of inadequacy that makes her say, unconsciously: "Nobody but nobody is going to make me hang up my clothes. I'll show my mother that if she's perfect, I don't want to be. I want to be just the opposite. I want to be myself, not my mother."

If people were motivated by sweet reason, counselors would be out of business. But the world is run on emotion, and the emotional life has to be unraveled before reason can take over and make sense.

So I knew that Nancy could not take my advice to forget herself, however brilliant she might be. Every nerve in her screamed, "The boys don't like you! The boys don't like you! The boys don't like you! Your mother will be calling soon to have you tell her—and maybe, in fantasy, yourself—that it isn't true. But you know it is. Is that the phone? Hello, Mother. Yes, I had a wonderful time at the dance. . . ."

I didn't get very far with Nancy. She didn't want to tell me whether or not she had spoken to her mother. I didn't try to find out. I wasn't sure that her mother could give up her illusion, no matter what her daughter said. We do not tear down the defenses of people until we are sure that they are ready to stand naked to the truth. Nancy herself may have sensed that it would be more disastrous to her to tell her mother the truth than to let the weaker person carry the lesser burden.

One night in March Nancy met a boy at a dance who was more lonely and miserable than she was. As far as I could tell they didn't dance at all. Every time I looked they were talking. He was a thin boy, narrow-shouldered, with a cowlick at the back of his head. She brought him over at the end of the dance.

"Sir, this is Joe Findlay. Joe, this is our headmaster and Mrs. Rutenber."

"It was nice to have you here, Joe," I said.

He nodded and mumbled, "Nice to be here."

For over a year, Joe came to see Nancy as often as he could get away from his own school. I don't know what they talked about, but I do know that Nancy abruptly stopped coming to my office to ask me why I believed in God.

I am sure that Joe was the better theologian.

Barbara

Overexpectation may come from the student herself. For some reason, usually one that she does not want to admit, she may be forcing herself toward goals that are not possible for her to achieve. She often tells herself that this is what her parents want of her, but she means that this is what she thinks her parents want of her, because she would want it if she were a parent. She is "projecting" her demands on herself as demands of the parents in order to blame the latter for any failures on her part. When she cannot meet her goals, the results may be serious—especially if she is unwilling to face the hidden motive.

Barbara came to us in the junior year, where she did an adequate C job in her various subjects. We felt that this was her academic capacity in a college preparatory setup, and were entirely pleased with her marks and her citizenship. She seemed to have made a good adjustment. She picked the same roommate and room for her senior year, was liked by the girls without being "popular" in the active sense, was cooperative in the dormitory—all in all a sound, likable, "nice" youngster, with no observable hang-ups.

A headmaster's report to a carefully chosen college would have read:

"Barbara is a girl of fine character, steady, reliable, friendly. She plugs steadily along, doing a wholly adequate, but certainly not outstanding, job in her various courses. I think she would do the same kind of work for you as she has for us, and you would find her an excellent and supporting citizen. Perhaps 'dependable' is the adjective most characteristic of her. She would not be distracted from her purpose of getting an education, and she would like to use it in some form of social service. As a member of the photography club. . . ."

Just an average student, and a nice average girl? The former may be possible with reservations, but there is no such thing as "a nice, average girl," or boy, or adult, for that matter—no matter how romantically Walt Whitman acclaims his "divine average."

In the senior year, after a good start, Barbara went to pieces. The teachers complained that she did not complete her homework assignments, always seemed sleepy, and appeared to be "far away" from class discussions. From the housemother I learned that she had become very apathetic, went to bed early, and found it difficult to get up in the morning. Her prefect reported that she had to be told again and again to do her "jobs" when her turn came.

"She doesn't seem like herself," she said. "I don't think she feels very well."

I didn't like the sound of any of it. The inability to function, the apathy, the sleepiness, the withdrawal were all classic signs of real depression. If unchecked, the depression could get worse. The dubious term "nervous breakdown" always leaps into the mind at a time like this, a high-wire phrase that to most people darkly promises a dramatic moment when something bursts inside of a person, causing her to climb the wall, or fight off the attendants from the sanitarium, or shoot herself.

Like most myths, this one dies hard. Periods of some depression among adolescents are common. They can even be helpful if they don't last too long and *if they mean that a young person is trying to live with a reality that she has managed to separate from a myth.* The real question is whether the person can function when she is depressed. That is the threshold of serious depression.

Barbara was not functioning. She was beginning to flunk, and I was asking the question at the bottom of all counseling: Why?

I talked to her parents, sensitive, intelligent people. They could give no answer. She had had a happy summer. The family seemed a close one. There had never been sibling rivalry that they had noticed.

I talked to her roommate, with Barbara's permission. She didn't understand it. Barbara had always been so studious. She just couldn't seem to study any more. She would open her books, stare at them, close them and go to bed. She was always sleepy.

I talked to the teachers in charge of her table. She wasn't stuffing—good. She wasn't starving—good. But she ate mechanically, as if she did it because it was the thing to do. She had stopped contributing to table conversation, and the teachers found it hard to draw her out, as I had asked them to try to do without being obvious about it.

And of course I talked to Barbara.

"I know, sir, I will flunk if I don't get to work, but I just don't seem to be able to do it. I don't seem to care whether I graduate or not, or whether I go to college, or whether I do anything. I just seem tired all the time."

"Well, Barbara, I do think you should have a physical

check-up, and your parents agree." Perhaps it was mono, but something told me it wasn't.

"Besides feeling tired, are you all right otherwise?" I was waiting for headaches, or pains in the stomach. I didn't want to suggest them. She didn't mention them.

"Well, sir, I really feel all right. I just don't seem to have any ambition."

"Are you in love, little one?" I smiled, and so did she.

"No, sir, nothing like that." The smile did not seem forced.

She continued to be sleepy and neglect her studies. The teachers complained. The doctor found no mono, no infection of any kind. I called her mother up.

"Mrs. Godfrey, I think I am over my head. I feel strongly that Barbara should see a psychiatrist or a psychiatric social worker. I think we've delayed long enough. I don't want to take the responsibility for her snapping out of this. I just cannot seem to get hold of any clue, and I have the strong feeling that she herself doesn't know, or won't admit to her conscious mind, the reasons for this depression."

I was relieved that they gave me permission to send her to a psychiatric social worker. I dissuaded them from taking her home to "build her up" unless they would get professional help for her.

"It started here," I said, "or at least revealed itself here. I'd like to see it solved here. If she goes home, I'm not at all sure she will come back. She likes the school, and she could feel a strong sense of failure if she went home. She doesn't need any failures; she needs the feeling of success. And that isn't going to come easily."

I wanted to give it one more try. Maybe I could pick up a clue with the Third Ear. In her case, somehow, I did not expect a dramatic development. I was more afraid that something was withering quietly away.

I called in the eight dormitory and three dining room prefects. I said to them, in confidence, a confidence which is almost never broken, that Barbara was upset—as they all knew—and that I couldn't find the reason.

"I want you to help me," I said. "There's something I'm missing. I want you to tell me everything you know about her except, of course, anything private that I would have no right to know. Don't feel that what you say is trivial. Most of it probably will be. Maybe she has an excessive love of peanut butter; maybe she only goes out with blond boys; maybe she believes in witchcraft; maybe she wishes she were five years old. Start talking."

The comments were unrevealing. Most of the information I already knew.

"Barbara is shy."

"Last year she worked hard, but this year she seems to have lost her ambition."

"Sometimes she talks a lot at the table, but this year she doesn't say much."

"She does like peanut butter, sir."

Everyone laughed.

"Go ahead," I said.

"She goes with a boy from her home town. I think she still goes with him."

"Yes," I said, "she told me that. I thought at first she might have broken up with him, but he was here last weekend, apparently. She says she likes him and they have had no trouble."

"She has four or five pictures of him on her dresser," one girl said.

"Those aren't her boyfriend," said another girl. "Those are pictures of her brother."

"Of her brother?" I asked. "Four or five pictures?"

"Oh, yes," said another girl. "She's crazy about her brother. Talks about him all the time. Much more than she does her boyfriend. You'd almost think *he* was her boy-friend."

A light switch clicked inside of me. Four pictures of her brother on her dresser. . . . "Tell me about her brother," I said.

"He's a doll," said the prefect of Barbara's dorm. "He came to the school last year to help her parents unpack the car. I would have been glad to have him unpack mine."

"Is he so good-looking?" I asked.

"He sure is," said the prefect, "and very cool, too."

"Cool" was the ultimate adjective at that time. It meant, of course, smooth, sophisticated.

It turned out that her brother was at Yale, a brilliant student. Later, I asked Barbara about him. Her eyes lit up, but I didn't believe them.

"Oh, he's terrific," she glowed. "I'm crazy about him. He's very smart and very popular, too. Everybody likes Jack. I'm so proud of him."

All of which, translated, really meant: "I hate my brother. He is so popular he makes me feel unloved. He is so smart he makes me feel dumb. Of course my parents are crazy about him. Who wouldn't be? Why couldn't I have had a different brother: a fair student, not too good-looking, shy, and barely able to get into college. Why did I have to have this son of a bitch? Why couldn't I be more like him?"

She went on to list his many qualities. She spoke as if he were a lover. She was so proud of him. They were so close. She just adored her brother. They could talk about anything with each other.

All of which, translated, meant: "I feel so guilty for hating him. It's a terrible thing to hate your own brother. He's never done anything to me. He can't help it if he's smarter and more attractive. Naturally my parents want me to be a better student than I am and more popular with everybody. They can't help it if they boast about him more than about me. Why would they boast about me, anyway? I'm jealous, I guess; that's all, just jealous. What kind of person is it who would be jealous of her own brother?"

Barbara would never have accepted the translations. She could not have accepted them and kept her self-image of the dear and loving sister. She had enough feelings of inferiority already. She could not bear to feel that she was morally inferior also by being jealous of her brother and hating him.

I talked to Barbara's parents, who at first refused to believe that Barbara was jealous of her brother and suddenly just couldn't "hack it" any more, as the girls expressed it. They were finally convinced, however, and all of us started a subtle campaign to build up her self-love and self-acceptance to the point where she could function. The parents were highly intelligent and found things to praise in her that were not in obvious competition with her brother's qualities.

Emotionally, she limped through the year and graduated, with faculty, parents, and administration all working toward that goal. We did not have time to come to grips with the defenses she had built up against her real feelings toward her brother. We worked for the replacement of her own sense of inferiority with a healthier and happier self-image, hoping this would be sufficient to get her back to performing. Sometimes that is enough; sometimes it isn't. In this case it was, at least for the time being. Sibling rivalry and jealousy are deep and disturbing, and often unacknowledged; but they come out somewhere at some time. They may have surfaced again in Barbara's later years. I don't know.

Parents and counselors need to listen with the Third Ear—before, not after, the child begins to act out her unacknowledged emotions, whether actively or, as in Barbara's case, passively to the point of withdrawal. Excessive praise can conceal even more excessive resentment.

Listening with the Third Ear is not an intuitive magic possessed only by professionals. It is a habit, and much of what is called intuition is also a habit. It is the habit of looking below the surface of action to the deeper springs of motive, while one remembers at the same time that motives are mixed and very often unconscious, and that people have a fascinating, dangerous, and almost unlimited ability to erect defenses against the truth about themselves, live behind those defenses, and confuse the stockade with its occupant.

7 Listening with the Third Ear: The Hidden Message

Actions as well as words need to be analyzed to see whether the student or daughter is trying to say something to somebody by what she *does*. She may not be talking to the school at all, by what she is doing in the school. She may be using the school as a means of conveying a message to someone outside the school, or to herself. And she may not herself realize what the message is.

Susan

Susan kept breaking minor rules. She was new that year, nearly sixteen, doing fairly well in her subjects. She had one of the friendliest smiles on the campus and always looked happy: a headmaster's delight, after all the droopy, homesick girls of the first few weeks.

But she kept breaking rules. The Dean reported that she always seemed contrite, and accepted with a very pleasant smile any bawling out, penalty, or patient explanation as to why the rule was made.

At the beginning, it was nothing more important than failing to sign out. The Dean explained that if a parent called, if there were some serious problem at home, perhaps involving her, we would know where she was, and probably when to expect her back if she were downtown. Reasons for this regulation or that were given. Susan smiled her bright, appreciative smile. Minor penalties were regretfully imposed. Susan continued to smile and was very cordial, almost affectionate.

The housemother reported that Susan was having difficulties with her roommate, and that the girls were on the side of the roommate. In the self-help system, where the girls take total care of their rooms, baths, halls, and common rooms, Susan did not do her share. The prefect in charge of inspection had no effect on her, but the prefect liked her. "She's a great kid," she told me. "She just can't seem to remember to do her jobs." My answer was short. "She'd remember if a five-dollar bill were attached to it, or a date with a very attractive boy!"

She began to cut morning assemblies, church, and classes from time to time. No sins, certainly, to evoke the Great White Throne (the young of this generation have never heard of the Great White Throne anyway, and the only judgment they know is to be grounded by their parents for staying out too late). Then she forged her mother's name to a weekend permission to go to Boston to visit a friend at Simmons. I sent for her.

"You wanted to see me, sir?"

"Yes, Susan, sit down." She looked poised, pleasant, a little apprehensive.

"Susan, I am told that you forged your mother's name to a permission slip for this weekend. Is that true?"

"Yes, it is," she said. "How did you find out?"

"The Dean was suspicious of two misspellings in a short note. One of them was Simmons with one m. The handwriting was good, but not that good."

She smiled—a warm, open smile. "I never could spell," she said. We both laughed.

"Let's talk a little bit about it. You must have been

sure your parents wouldn't call you or the school this weekend."

"That's right. My father had to make a business trip to California, and my mother went with him."

"You arranged, of course, for a friend to mail this note from your home town?"

"Yes, sir." She is beginning to be uncomfortable with her role as plotter. I want her to be. There is no edge in my voice, no anger. I hope the anger will eventually come from *her*—at herself.

"You don't have to answer this next question. I'm only interested in you—not some stranger. However, since you're the one that planned this, I'd like to know whether your friend at Simmons—I assume her invitation was genuine—knew that you were pulling this trick. I assure you I will not act against her in any way."

"No, sir, she didn't. On my word of honor." She is becoming upset.

"I accept your word of honor."

She said nothing. Everything is very low key. Few people have been screamed into heaven.

"Let's talk a little more. When did your parents leave for California?"

"Monday."

"Why didn't you have your mother write a note in advance?"

"She had told me she wouldn't give me any weekend permissions until my marks improved."

"Was your father in this decision, too?"

"Oh, I guess so. He usually goes along with whatever Mother says."

"Do you get along well with your mother, Susan?"

She seemed to come to life. Her face brightened. "Oh, yes," she said. "I think Mother is a terrific person. Most of my friends don't get along with their mothers, but I have always been very close to mine."

"What about your father?"

"Well, Daddy is very smart, of course. He's very busy with the plant. But he's very good to all of us."

"And what about your brothers and sisters? You're the oldest, aren't you? Who comes next, and next, and next?"

"My brother is two and a half years younger than I am; Marcia is ten; and Tim, the baby, is five."

"How about your thirteen-year-old brother? Do you get along with him well?"

She laughed. "Oh, I get mad at him sometimes; but we get along pretty well. Marcia is very quiet, unlike Stephen. Of course we all adore Tim. I guess we shouldn't call him the baby. He'll be going to school in a year."

I remember the family as an affectionate, happy, outgoing group. We are always pleased when parents bring all the children. The mother was the spokesman. She was very attractive-looking, and so was Susan. The father was sure of himself, obviously successful financially, but not as warm as the mother.

We came back to the forged note: "Susan, when you put your signature to something, you're putting your whole life into it, your character, the kind of person you are. When your parents, or perhaps you, sign a check, you are proclaiming to the whole world, 'I have money in the bank to cover this check.' And people believe you. They have to. If no one trusted anyone's word—a signature, a promise, a statement of fact—society would stop. MacDuffie would stop. Industry, service professions, the law, even the ministry, would be bankrupt. When you signed your name to that note, you said to everyone in the community: 'This is my mother's name. This is her permission. I guarantee it with my whole self, with my me-ness, with the reputation I want to have, and all the values for which I stand.' But it wasn't true. It was dishonest."

Tears were beginning to come to her eyes. I had knocked her down, and I felt bad. Now I wanted to pick her up. But not too quickly. "Little one," I said, and I can't apologize for a phrase that is part of the history of the school, "I know you didn't think of all those things. You just wanted to take a weekend, in any way you could, and you saw the way. It's my job to point out the implications. I do it for myself, too.

"If it hadn't been for the misspellings, the note would never have been questioned, because we assume the girls are honest. We assume that they tell the truth unless we have evidence to the contrary. And even then, if we can't prove it, we ask you whether or not you lied. If you say you didn't, that's the end of it. We don't ask you, 'Are you *sure* you didn't?' We trust you. Do you like that kind of school, Susan?"

"Of course I do," she answered, almost belligerently.

"So does every other girl at MacDuffie. But if you want a school that trusts you, you have to be trustworthy. You cannot say: 'How nice of RDR to assume that we are honest. That will give me a chance to forge my mother's name and get my weekend. I like a school that trusts me. It makes it so much easier to get away with things. I'm glad that no one checks at church to see whether I've gone or not. I'll sign out, of course, but I won't go.' "

She was silent.

"When you are not trustworthy, you are saying: 'This school is naive to have a trust system or honor system. It is foolish for the school to believe that girls won't try to get away with things. The school should check us out more carefully, be suspicious of what we say, follow us to be sure we really go to town and not somewhere off limits, look through our drawers, smell our breaths, try to catch us breaking a rule.' Let me ask you a question. Suppose there had been no misspelling to create suspicion in the Dean's mind. Suppose she had just automatically taken your note, studied it, brought out another from your mother and compared the handwriting. How would you have felt during all this? Wouldn't you have been indignant? Wouldn't you have said, 'She doesn't trust me'? Wouldn't that have made you angry and resentful?"

"Yes, sir, I know I would have been furious. I'm really very sorry that I cheated. I never thought of it this way."

The "you ought" has become the "I ought." The rest is anticlimax.

"I know you're sorry. And I want you to know that you haven't dropped in my high opinion of you. I think you're an honest person who did a dishonest thing. I have to punish you, but I don't think you need any punishment to keep you from being dishonest again. However, I'm sure you understand that I have to say something to the school when a thing like this happens. I can't say: 'If a girl is genuinely sorry about what she's done there will be no penalty. But if I don't think she is sorry, I'm going to punish her.'

"In the first place, I might be wrong. But in the second place, the world just isn't like this. Acts do have consequences, sometimes the same ones, whether the person is sorry about them or not. I have to give the same penalty to the girl who feels sorry she did it and to the girl who only feels sorry that she has been caught. But I make that distinction in my own mind between the two girls. And I'll tell your parents that I make that distinction. I hope it's important to you that I do."

"Yes, sir, it is; and thank you very much. Am I going to be suspended?"

"Would you think it fair if I did?"

"Yes, I would—if it weren't for too long."

We both smiled.

"I'm not going to suspend you. You didn't really get your weekend. But I'm going to take away certain privileges, and I'm going to put you on probation for five weeks. Probation is not a penalty here; it's a condition. It says, 'Any important rule broken during this period will make you liable to stronger punishment than you would otherwise get.' But I'm not worried that you will break the probation. I'm just making a statement to the rest of the school. I think you've been here long enough to know that I never actually announce any penalty, except to the faculty. And you don't have to say anything to anyone about this meeting. That is up to you. It won't come from me. One more thing. You're sorry, here in my office with me. I don't expect you to go around the dorm in sackcloth and ashes. You did something; I did what I had to do. The incident is over, and we start again with each other as if it had never happened. But please don't go out into the dormitory and become a hero to the other girls, especially the young ones. I hope you'll be true to what you *really* think. That's all I'm asking. Is that fair?"

"Yes, it is. And thank you again."

She smiled and left the room. I leaned back with a sense of peace. I thought the turning point had come. I knew the parents would back me up. I have only had one or two in thirty-one years who didn't. But the battle wasn't over. There is more than one kind of reality.

For five weeks, Susan was a model boarder. Her grades improved, and I was pleased to take her off probation.

A short time later she signed up to go downtown, did not return for dinner, nor for lights-out. We called her parents to tell them she had disappeared. The night watchman found her trying to climb the fire escape into her room at midnight. We notified her parents that she had returned and that I would report the circumstances in the morning.

But I came down to the dorm as soon as I heard from the housemother.

"Well, hi," were my first words.

"Hi," she answered.

"I wanted to come down to tell you I was glad you returned. I'll talk to you at length in the morning."

"Do my parents know that I was away from the school?"

"Yes. When you weren't in your room for evening study hours, we checked the other dormitories. We found you had not come back to dinner. No one seemed to know where you were. So we called home and said you had disappeared. They decided not to call the police."

"The police!" She seemed amazed that the possibility of calling the police had even been considered.

"Why, yes, the police. You seem surprised." (They usually are. They are young. Nothing bad can happen to them.)

"I never dreamed you'd call the police." She seemed aggrieved.

"Look," I said, "What do you think I've been doing all night. Resting? At 8:15, I went through the classroom building and the gym. The Dean and the housemothers were checking the dorms. The night watchman was combing the campus. By the time we called your parents, we had checked out every bus terminal in Springfield, as well as the train. Had they seen anyone who looked like you boarding the bus? Where were you going?

"All your parents had to do was to ask us to alert the police and your name and description would have been teletyped all over the East, anyway. Then a reporter checks the police record and your name gets in all the newspapers. The reporter calls me up at, say, 2:00 A.M. and asks a question like this:

" 'Why was the girl sent to your school?' Of course I answer, 'To get the best possible education.'

"I already know what the *next* question will be. Here it is in one form or another:

" 'Was this girl fond of boys?' During the Second World War, the reporter would have asked, 'Did she like sailors and soldiers? Do you think maybe she picked someone up?' The girl in question had taken an earlier train home for a weekend without notifying her parents, arrived home to find that they had gone to meet her in Albany, and promptly went to bed and to sleep. What should I have said, Susan, if the reporter had asked me whether you liked boys? He is not just inquiring into your happy normality. He is inferring that maybe you ran off with a lover. It would make a good headline: 'Girl from Exclusive School (we're always "exclusive" in the tabloids, and "rich" of course) Runs Away with Sailor, or Soldier, or College Boy. Found in Motel Love Nest,' the reporter hopes."

Susan said nothing.

"You haven't really leveled with me. Somehow I don't see you as a person who has to break the rules in order to feel independent of the establishment. Something, someone is bothering you, is bugging you. Who is it?"

"It's nobody," she said, but with less conviction than usual.

"Is it me?" (Although you believe in the nominative case, you don't say "Is it I" at this moment in history.)

"No, sir, it's nothing." She was trying to sound light, but it didn't quite come off.

"Is it your roommate?"

"No."

"Is it anyone at the school?"

"No. Really it's no one. I just get these impulses!"

"Are you sure it isn't anyone at home?"

"Oh, no, I tell you it's nobody." She was beginning to look bright-faced again. The girls call it "plastic."

I was tired, irritable, licked. One more try, and I'll go home. I forced the anger out of my voice. I pleaded.

"Look, Susan, please, tell me. Tell me what's bugging you. What are you mad at? Whom are you mad at? What's the trouble? Tell me, tell me; come on, it's late, tell me. I know it's something. Tell me. Tell me what's the matter."

It was 1:00 A.M.

The soft face hardened; the mouth was an open scar. And then the scream:

"It's my mother! I hate her! I hate her! She's so beautiful she makes me ugly!"

And the flood came.

What do you say to the mother, who is indeed a svelte and lovely-looking woman? And charming besides.

Do you tell her to become a little plump like her daughter? Wear unattractive clothes? Look more like a Mom making that good old apple pie, or Whistler's mother?

You can fit human behavior into tight little frames of reference and show off your knowledge of orthodox psychology. You can say with the ready authority of the doctrinaire that of course the mother and daughter are competing for the love of the father, who is very busy with the business of securing them the wherewithal with which to compete. Unconsciously, of course, all around.

But a person is never the sum total of the theories about her, however important the analysis may be. The girl slips out of the theory as often as she slips into it. We believe in analysis, but we are not analysts; we have learned much from psychology, motivational and behavioristic, but we are not psychologists; our minds may be oriented toward psychiatry, but we are not doctors. We cannot wait until all the evidence is in, the research completed, and the results beatified by the brotherhood.

It is 1:30 A.M. in the dormitory of a school for girls. Susan has stopped crying at last, with what guilt, fear, release, shame still clinging to her, I do not know. I shall deliver myself of the least profound but perhaps the most therapeutic words I can think of:

"Little one, go to bed."

They say that "only the soul that knows the mighty griefs can know the mighty raptures." But the mighty griefs and the mighty raptures alike end up with shredded wheat and coffee in the morning. Morning is one of the great realities. No school can survive without it.

I talked to the father and the mother. I talked about the goal, and only grazed what might have been the underlying problems. To have discussed them too intimately, except by indirection, might have brought about too much self-consciousness—and new defenses against an unpleasant realization. It might have made each of them too analytical about themselves. I wanted them to forget themselves and concentrate on Susan—and keep concentrating. I cannot solve their problems, but I may help Susan solve hers. I live with her every day, for over eight months a year.

The goal is to build up her self-image; to make her feel as attractive as she is, or could be; to make her accept herself with pleasure but without too much self-loving concern; to convince her that her father thinks she's terrific (he'd better tell her so, or she'll marry the first cub who does); to make her proud of her mother without comparing herself to her; and to make both her father and mother face some of the realities about bringing up children. You never take them for granted; you praise and encourage them; you give them as much attention as you possibly can, which does not mean as many gifts as you can afford; and both you, and the school, try through the values you believe in (do you?) to turn her gaze outward rather than inward.

And since adolescents of all people are looking for models after whom they can pattern their sometimes chaotic lives, we might echo Mr. Dooley's addition to Scripture, "Bring up a child in the way he should go, and, *walk there yourself once in a while.*"

I talked to Susan many times after that, usually about inconsequential things, just to keep communication open. We checked quietly with the parents from time to time. Unknown to Susan we gave her responsibilities whenever we could, without seeming to have thought about it. She finished MacDuffie and college without further incident. The smile became less automatic, more expressive of genuine pleasure. I haven't seen her since but wrote her a note when she got married. You do not ask for long letters of gratitude, fervent expressions of appreciation. You are grateful for opportunity. People talk about the "real" world outside of school. It's a myth. If the real world wasn't there in the early morning for Susan, where was it?

8 Listening with the Third Ear: Translations and Role-Playing

It is obvious that the parent and teacher must not only listen with the Third Ear but be able to translate what he or she hears. There is often more than one translation possible; seemingly obvious translations may be incorrect; and some translations may come too late to prevent the young person from acting out some hidden frustration. I shall give examples of all three of these possibilities, among others.

"I hate this school," a girl may say to me. Since I have committed my life to the school, my first impulse is to say: "Well, look, sweetie, we're not so crazy about you either. If you don't like it here, you can always go somewhere else."

Tempting? Yes, of course. But it would be a disastrous answer.

In the first place "we're not so crazy about you either" is saying that we are the school, and she isn't. But she is the school, too. You might even be able to explain that to her. It is worth a try.

I remember a girl arriving at the station years ago. She had never seen the school; she didn't want to go away to school anyway; and she did not greet me as if I were her long lost surrogate father.

"You're Rosalind Hunter," I said. "I'm Dr. Rutenber."

"How do you do?" she said perfunctorily, adding, "I hate to be called 'Rosalind.' Would you mind calling me Andy."

"Is that your middle name?" I asked, making conversation.

"My middle name is Andrews," she said in an accusing tone, as if I should have figured it out. "Everybody calls me Andy."

"The car is over here, Andy," I said. "Do your parents call you Andy?"

"*Everybody* calls me Andy," she repeated, as if she didn't want to have to tell me again.

I resisted a momentary desire to call her "Rosalind" by mistake, and we started for the school.

"I didn't even know I was going away to school until my father told me he'd been looking at schools and had chosen this one. He seems to think I need to be challenged more. What's this school like anyway?" she said.

"I don't know what it's like," I answered.

She looked at me in surprise. "You don't know what it's like?" she repeated. "Aren't you the headmaster?"

"I don't know what it's like because I don't know what you're like," I said. "You're the school, you know—you and the other girls. You'll be helping to create the school as soon as you step into Main House. What kind of school do you want it to be?"

"Not too hard," she said, and we both laughed.

That was the beginning of a friendship that is still a close one. She was one of the girls who in the early struggling days of our tenure helped to shape the school.

We were talking about the Third Ear, and the girl who says, "I hate the school."

She may mean many things by that remark. She may mean: "I hate the school because I don't think you like me, and I'm going to tell you off before you get to me."

She may mean: "I hate the school because I feel unimportant in it. I'm no great scholar, or athlete, or leader. I'm nobody and nothing in this school. To hell with it."

She may mean: "I miss Charlie's arms around me, holding me tight. His kisses. The excitement of being with him and near him. The gang of kids back home. The times we've had."

I hear somebody saying: "Well, Mr. Headmaster, she may just hate the school. Period. Maybe it's not as great to her as it is to you. Maybe it isn't great at all."

Maybe not. But that isn't the real question. She's *in* the school, just as she's in her own family, whether she wants to be or not, whether she likes it or not, whether or not she would like to be somewhere else.

She's one of ours, and we have a commitment to her and to her parents, and to the rest of the students, too. But especially to her.

We cannot accept the philosophy of "Period." It is a word with cold feet and a closed heart. It predicates an end in a world that is always beginning again—and again. It seizes the symptom and thinks it has found the cause. A cowardly word, spoken with bold assurance. Go no further, or deeper. This is it.

"She may just hate the school. Period." There is no such thing as "just hates"; "just stubborn"; "just good"; "just bad"; "just cooperative"; "just a pain in the neck."

There are reasons behind these descriptions of personality, attitudes, and actions. Period. And when we find these reasons, we may be able to persuade the student— or son, or daughter—that she is liked, or loved, as the case may be; that the school or home needs her, as she needs the opportunity to feel important and necessary to the community; and that Charlie's arms around her, however exciting, cannot hold her upright for twenty-four hours or days or months: that other experiences and excitements, even breakfast, must come between them.

Alice

She is facing me in the office with an unpleasant look on her face. She is a full scholarship boarding student, which means that the school is investing considerable money in her four-year education.

She starts right in.

"I'm very disappointed with this school. It is really quite different from the way it was represented to me."

My blood pressure goes up—quietly, I hope.

"Well, Alice, just what are you disappointed about?"

"Well, you told me that you had a wonderful faculty, but I don't think it is so wonderful. I'm often bored in class."

She has touched another nerve. We have the best faculty in the United States. I'd go to jail before I'd say otherwise.

Even after years of this kind of conversation, I think how delicious it would be to say the first thing that comes to my mind.

Such as: "If you're so disappointed with the school and its faculty, why don't you look for another school, public or private? I'll give you a fine recommendation." You linger on the "fine recommendation." You want it to sink in.

Or: "You're bored, did you say? My goodness, gracious. We can't have a MacDuffie student bored for one moment. I'll tell the faculty that if they can't make *hic, haec, hoc* exciting, they can look for a job somewhere else."

Or (with great dignity, cold eyes, and a hard, flat voice): "Well, Alice, I certainly want to give as much help as I can, and I certainly am not expecting the students to tell me how wonderful the school is, or to put an apple on my desk every day (the light touch). On the other hand (now we're getting down to the nitty-gritty), I really don't think I should be asked to subsidize discontent. If you feel that this faculty is not up to your requirements, I am sure you would be happier with a different group of teachers, somewhere else."

But of course I don't say any of these things. We are teachers first and administrators second, and we have a commitment to young people. Hopefully, we have learned to translate.

Translated, Alice is telling me that her scholarship makes her feel inferior. She is receiving, not giving. I am the donor, so I am in the superior position.

She can elevate herself and get back at me by telling me in effect that what I am giving her isn't so much after all; that she's ready to throw it away (she isn't!); that she sees through it (she knows a top faculty when she sees it); that she hasn't been taken in by the establishment, the one on top, the power structure. The establishment cannot fool her or buy her off with scholarship money.

"The expectation of gratitude is mean, and is continually punished by the total insensibility of the obliged person," says Emerson. But then he adds, "We can receive anything from love, for that is a way of receiving it from ourselves."

So we sit face to face in my office, and I know I must love her, though at that moment I feel far from loving.

We are so afraid of being hypocrites that we shrink from practicing love before we feel it. So we only practice the dislike we feel. And we dislike still more. Practice makes perfect.

I must speak softly, though I don't yet feel soft. I must throw the stick of my power away; and of her obligation. It is an effort to say it.

"I'm sorry you feel that way about the faculty, Alice. I am very sure you are wrong. I think you will discover that this is a group of superb teachers. I can't accept your belief that I misrepresented the school. Think it over, won't you? And thanks for coming in."

We are hardly close to one another, but she has had her chance to irritate me; we have talked horizontally, not vertically; I have not retreated nor has she. It has been a talk among equals. She has kept her self-respect. I have not mentioned a scholarship. If you're going to give a scholarship or anything else, give it out of love—some kind of love, anyway. The expectation of gratitude is mean, and no one likes to be forever kneeling.

When I was a boy, I had an experience that I did not fully understand at the time.

I had just learned to swim, and in Walden, New York, where we were living, a narrow and I am sure thoroughly polluted river, the Walkill, flowed through the town. In the arrogance of my new skill, I tried to swim across the Walkill one Saturday afternoon.

My strength gave out and maybe fifty yards from the shore I had to call for help. A boy I knew named Tony came to my rescue, gave me a powerful push toward the shore, swam up to give me another and another as I kept sinking, until my feet hit bottom. Gasping for breath, I staggered up to the bank and lay down.

When I could talk, I said, "Thanks, Tony," but I remember to this day that I didn't feel as grateful toward him as I knew I should. All the way home, I kept saying to myself, "He saved my life. Why do I feel rather angry with him? What's the matter with me, anyway? He saved my life."

I know now why I did not feel as grateful as I should have. Tony was the savior, the hero, the overcomer. I was the pathetic, nearly drowned rat who staggered up the bank. I was prostrate, gagging—and deeply humiliated.

All the boys and girls were watching Tony save me.

He was at the top, and I at the bottom. He was the

donor, I the receiver of his athletic prowess, his superior swimming skill, his lifesaving act. Admiring glances for him; a pitying concern for me.

I'm grateful to him now, anyway.

Kay

The President of the Senior Class has come to see me. I know that she is a fine person and is very fond of the school. On the other hand, she is president of the class, and it is her bounden duty to tell me every once in a while what I'm doing wrong and what the girls want me to do. She is a fourth quarter student but a top 1 percent girl.

We go through the usual complaints and the annual request that the seniors be excused from final examinations. Then she speaks with somewhat more intensity.

"Sir, there is one thing I would like to talk about, and a number of the girls feel the same way as I do. That's this business about 100 percent of the girls being accepted at college every year. There was a piece about it in the paper the other day. Some of the girls wonder if this school isn't just interested in its image ('image' was a wicked word in the late sixties—almost as bad as 'structure'). It seems as if all the school is interested in is getting 100 percent of its girls accepted at college."

"Are you implying that that's all I'm interested in?"

"Well, it would seem so."

"You think it would be better if I could say that all of the girls tried for college and 85 percent were accepted? Would you want to be one of the 15 percent turned down?"

"Well, no, I wouldn't, but I hate to see the 100 percent emphasized so much, as if that were the most important thing in the school."

She has been at MacDuffie for four years. She knows that I spend most of my time talking to the students about themselves; arguing, discussing, building up their confidence as women as well as persons; telling them what I think is right or wrong; listening to their troubles; comforting them; hopefully, giving them the courage to be and to do. She knows that we never print or announce an honor roll, except once a year in the newspapers to remind the city that we are here. She knows I am interested in the girl, not where she goes to college. But she wants me to say so; she wants it confirmed. Why?

I decide that this may be a little more personal than merely pitting student ideas against mine.

Translated, she is really saying to me, Sir, I have been here four years. I have found it difficult to settle down to books. I haven't been much of a student. Athletics I have loved and being president of my class junior year and senior year.

Suddenly, I wonder whether maybe you think I'm kind of a failure. This *is* an academic school, and I haven't been academic. Most of the girls are much brighter than I. Oh, I made a four-year college and you told my parents it was just as accredited as a college could be; but everyone knows it's an easy one.

I guess I'm not sure whether or not I'm a flop. Tell me that academics aren't that important; tell me that I'm successful and have helped you with the school. Tell me that if a person didn't make any college at all, you wouldn't care as long as she tried.

I told her.

Carolyn

Often you are fooled by thinking that you understand a person by the way she talks and acts in public.

Carolyn talked incessantly. No one else could get a word in edgewise at the table. You would pass her in the corridor, smiling and talking to some girl who was never responding. She couldn't. If her companion started to say something, Carolyn would interrupt gaily with something else she wanted to say.

She was a pleasant girl, with energy overflowing, always happy—and talking. A moment's silence at the table could not last if Carolyn were there. It had to be filled with chatter.

She was very good-natured. If a girl told her to let someone else say something, in the blunt idiom of the young, she would say, "I'm sorry." You felt that she really was. But even while she was saying she was sorry, you knew by the brightness of her eye and the tilt forward of her head that she was about to let loose a new barrage of words.

I had driven my car one night to pick up five girls at a dance at a nearby boys' school.

The girls came out in the usual after-prom excitement, and as they settled down I asked, "How was the dance?"

Carolyn jumped into the question mark and proceeded to rattle off her impressions of the dance, the boys, the music, the chaperones. She was very animated and her eyes were bright, and no one else had a chance.

I lost my temper and interrupted, "Carolyn, *please*, let somebody else talk."

"I'm sorry," she said pleasantly, but the smile was a little forced this time. I felt sorry that I had corrected her in public and hurt her feelings.

The other girls started to talk; Carolyn seemed to brighten in a moment; and I decided I had hardly grazed her ego.

The next night she came in to see me. For a moment she smiled brightly and started to talk. Suddenly, she started to sob, and I thought she would never stop. Her shoulders were shaking and she couldn't get her breath. I stood up and patted her on the shoulder: "Go ahead and cry, as long as you want. Get it out of your system."

She was finally calmer and sat there wiping her nose. I waited, handing her a box of Kleenex.

"What's the matter with me?" she demanded and

started to cry again. She reached for another tissue. When the words came, they came fast.

"I know I talk all the time. I know it. I know it! I know it!! You don't have to tell me (the tone was belligerent, but it changed quickly). Nobody has to tell me. I'm a fool. I know that, too. But, sir, sir, don't you understand. I'm scared! I'm scared to death. I'm so scared I could run out of this school tonight and run and run and run until I dropped dead." She was sobbing again, and I waited.

"You don't have to be scared any more," I said, "and you don't have to run any more. I'm sorry I didn't understand, but you're home now. Remember—you don't have to be scared any more."

"How can I help it?" she asked tearfully. "Why do I feel I have to keep every conversation going? Why do I talk and laugh like an ape all the time? The kids think I'm a weirdo, and I am, but why? why?"

"Carolyn, at this moment, do you feel scared?"

"No, I really don't. But I was scared to come to see you. I almost didn't come," she admitted.

She was beginning to calm down. She smiled uncertainly. It was as if she had suddenly realized she didn't have to talk. I looked at her curiously. How little we really know people, I thought. The brash, loud, insistent, loquacious Carolyn I thought I knew, the girl whose ego was so big that she didn't care who wanted to talk, *she* was going to hold the floor, was suddenly quiet and rather crushed.

"Why don't we just sit here for a few minutes," I said, "and relax."

She smiled and said nothing, but her body was tense. She was tapping her middle finger on the arm of the chair.

"Carolyn," I said, "what are you scared about? You surely do hide it well. I would have said you weren't afraid of anything—or anybody. Tell me about it, won't you?"

"I've always talked a lot," she said brightly.

"I didn't ask you if you always talked a lot. I asked you why you were scared."

"I'm not really a timid person. You know that."

"I want to know why you're scared."

"I'm not really scared, sir; you're making a good deal out of nothing." Her tone was critical, irritated. "What have I got to be scared of?"

"Little one, you said you were scared to death. I thought maybe you talked all the time to cover up some fear, perhaps a fear that someone will ask you a question you don't want to answer if you should stop talking, and there was a pause."

She looked at me with horror—there is no other word to describe it. If I hadn't known her, I would have thought she had committed a crime.

"Who told you?" she asked.

"Nobody has told me anything—anything at all. I have no idea what it is that has made you so unhappy. If it's something that would make me send you home, I don't want to hear it; and I'll send you to a counselor outside the school. If it's just something that upsets you terribly, I'd like to know what it is." I spoke very softly, "What is it, Carolyn? What is it? You don't have to be afraid to tell me."

She looked as if she were going to burst into tears again.

"I don't want you to cry any more," I said. "I want you to tell me."

I spoke briskly, matter-of-factly, with just an edge of insistence. She took a deep breath, as if gathering herself together, and replied almost in the same tone.

"It's my brother," she said quietly, although with obvious effort. "He—he's not all there. He's severely retarded."

She looked up to see how I was taking the news.

"That's too bad," I said. "Is he in an institution?"

"No, he's home. My mother won't send him to an institution, although the doctor says she ought to. My mother feels guilty about Jimmy, as if she were responsible for him. He's hard to take care of. He can't do anything much for himself, and he's strong. When my mother looks at him sometimes, she starts to cry; and then my father gets very angry at Mother and swears and throws his paper down and goes out of the room. My mother doesn't have much time for me, and I understand why. But sometimes I wish she would fuss over me the way she fusses over Jimmy. And I get jealous—and then I hate myself, because Jimmy is my brother, and my twin. I try to love him. I take him out and play with him in the yard, but he looks so funny that all the kids stare at him and I feel ashamed of him, and I hate myself because I do."

In my mind, I finished the story while sobs shook her again. She had come to boarding school and all the girls were talking about their brothers and their sisters; and she knew that someone was going to ask her if she had any brothers and sisters and she would either have to lie or tell them about Jimmy, and she couldn't bear to do either, so she talked and talked and talked so no one could break into her torrent of words and ask her,

"Carolyn, do you have any brothers or sisters?"

Role Playing and Rebellion

One of the reasons why the generation gap is wider than it needs to be is the unwillingness of adults to realize one of the basic facts of adolescent psychology: role playing.

Like the Greek god Janus, the adolescent is facing two ways at the same time, looking back toward childhood and forward toward adulthood. To use that much overworked phrase, "identity crisis," the adolescent does not yet know who he is. Certainly, in many cases, he is not an integrated person. He is trying out different roles; he must continually test himself and the environment to find out what is reality and what is myth. And what is reality and what is myth inside of him.

He is also living up to the expectations of the peer group and of society in general. It is axiomatic that young people should rebel against the establishment. Everyone is in favor of this rebelliousness, as long as it is directed toward someone else.

I don't claim to be an exception, but, psychologically, as a parent and a headmaster, I must accept the fact that the only way young people can develop a strong ego-structure is to test themselves against the older generation, its ideas and its institutions. This is not a frightening experience if only adults would stop being frightened. (I am of course not referring to the physical violence of the sixties, which I cannot possibly condone even though I believe that it escalated in proportion to the palpable timidities of the educational establishment.) Young people cannot test themselves on mush. They cannot earn their spurs against weakness or overcome opponents who are already lying down. They expect—they even want—to believe that the adult generation has definite values, beliefs, convictions. They are not about to accept them: they need to question and argue and present an opposite view. How else can they arrive at their own convictions and develop that inner strength we call character? The fact that the contact between the two generations is necessarily abrasive at times is no proof of a wide and threatening generation gap.

The parent who finds any opposition from his child threatening is acknowledging his own lack of confidence in what he believes and lives. The child is sometimes pleased, always surprised, and usually distressed, to discover that he has that much power over an adult or group of adults. He needs to feel that however fragmented and confusing his own adolescence may be, there is a world of stability, maturity, and conviction which he is about to join. He will question that world for two reasons: one, because it is comforting to know that it is there (if it is); and two, because he is a young person and young people are supposed to question everything. It is a role to which they have been assigned by all the writers, the media, the clerics, the sociologists—and of course by their own self-conscious peer group. Every adult in contact with young people will be quizzed and contradicted, indicted and angered, by what logic the young can command (about equal to that of the old) and what emotion they can summon up.

Psychologists tell us that criminals act as criminals are expected to act, developing a subculture with its own orthodoxies of dress, manner, and behavior. Ministers in the early part of the century acted or appeared to act as Men of God were supposed to. Clergymen of today are predictably different from their predecessors but very much like each other as they embrace the secular city and all of its current orthodoxies. If a young clergyman gets up to give a talk before young people, most of the adults present and probably the boys and girls themselves could write the speech before they hear it. And doubtless headmasters are not exceptions. The younger generation is supposed to rebel. It is the job of the adult to understand and accept this role, put limitations on its excesses, but always be willing to sit down and discuss whatever problem or question has been presented with respect for the girl's opinion, understanding of her point of view, but not necessarily agreement with its substance.

As parents and teachers we must reject the modern myth that to express a conviction is to impose it. We can impose public conduct, but in a free society we cannot impose belief. That does not mean we should not express it. We have to learn not to stand above our adolescents but with them; however, we should never trade our convictions for their easy and faintly contemptuous applause and never abdicate our responsibilities as parents and teachers in order to promote an uneasy and fictitious peace. We must believe passionately but realistically that the generation gap can be partially bridged, but that we cannot break into the tight circle of the peer group if we try to tiptoe in with apology or crash through with denunciation. They must feel our own self-confidence, our respect for them, and our affection.

It is the winter of 1968. Added to the wholly normal internal pressures on the adolescent to question the adult world and play the role of youth in rebellion is the Vietnam War—focal point of the sharpest and most violent revolution of young people in our generation. When I say "play the role" I do not mean the word "play" to connote any dilettantism in the attitude of young people, any idea that they were merely "acting" without sincere purpose and genuine feeling. Certainly the young men who faced the draft and possible death in Vietnam had something very personal to protest about: their lives. And the girls who loved them joined in this rebellion. "Where Have All the Young Men Gone" was the haunting question, expressed in a moving song.

The fact that the war in Vietnam greatly exacerbated the rebellious spirit of youth at a given time in our history does not alter the enduring reality of adolescent challenge to the authority of the older generation and to its values. We should accept these challenges as normal and should answer them seriously, calmly, and with what wisdom, understanding, and humor we can muster.

It is a week before November 15, 1968, target date of a nationwide Moratorium called by various groups. Workers have been urged to leave their jobs and students their schools to gather in public places and hear speakers denounce the war. A dark shawl of violence is fluttering over the country.

At MacDuffie, the great majority of girls have signed a petition asking that school be called off for that day so they can go to town and hear the speakers in the public square.

"You'd better let them go," says one of the teachers, "or they'll go anyway."

I know that I'm not going to let them go. If anything happens to them, if a girl is injured, it is I who have to call up an anguished parent to explain that her daughter is in the hospital because of a permission, fraught with some danger, that I gave to her and to her fellow students. The buck stops with the headmaster, and he is very aware of it.

I shall need to explain this very carefully to the students. They will not agree, of course; they will be angry and feel that they are being treated like babies. But it is important for them to feel that they have been heard respectfully; they have been talked to like adults even if they think they have been treated like children. It is vital that they consider that *you have reasons for your decision that are important to you*, reasons which they can respect while they vehemently disagree with them. The assent of the young person to your fairness, your consistency, your genuine concern for her will prevent in most cases the angry confrontations that are so disturbing to adults. Even in a time of angry confrontations. If the confrontation does occur, you *assume*, whether it is one person or a group, that they will accept your decision. Your assumption cannot be based on a smug belief in your superior age and wisdom. That will shine through whatever you say like the morning sun. It is rather based on an appeal to their own adulthood; their own sense of fairness; and their own understanding of the problems you face.

"Sir, may I see you?"

"Sure, come on in."

Brenda is a new girl, tall, intense, very bright. She is

pretty in a way that says, Don't tell me I'm pretty. I have more important things on my mind than my looks.

I think I know why she's there.

"Sit down, Brenda, won't you?"

She sits down but does not relax.

"I'm sorry," she says, with the tears beginning to come, "but I just do not feel that I can go to school on November 15. All the girls are very upset."

Twenty years ago I would probably have told her she would either go to class or pick up her bag and go home. But headmasters grow up, too.

"I don't want to talk about 'all the girls,' " I said. "I want to talk about you since you've come to see me. I respect your point of view and your strong feelings about the war. Do you have someone in Vietnam from your family?"

"No, I don't," she said shortly, "although I know a boy from high school who is there. I just think we ought to be allowed to go. I just feel I have to go."

"I tried to explain my reasons for saying 'no' this morning at assembly. I respect your reasons for wanting to go, and I think you should respect my reasons for thinking that I can't take the responsibility of letting you do it."

"But can't we ever make our own decisions?" she demanded angrily.

"You make your own decisions all the time," I answered. "You make decisions every time you are on a date, or offered a drug, or decide to goof off instead of study. But there are some decisions in this community that I have to make—and I have tried to explain why this is one of them."

"I just don't feel I can stay in school on that day." The tone is belligerent.

"Brenda," I said, "you really have no business putting me on this kind of spot. What you're really asking me to do is make an exception in your case. But I don't believe you want me to get up in assembly tomorrow and say to 300 other girls: 'None of you can go downtown on Moratorium day except Brenda Moore. She feels so strongly about it that I am letting her go.' You wouldn't want me to say that, and I certainly couldn't say it. I expect you to join the common lot and be at your classes, like everyone else. And thank you."

She didn't thank me. She walked out bitterly, and with tears.

But on November 15 she was going to her classes as pleasantly as everyone else. No one skipped; there were no further protests. Brenda had shown her independence of my point of view and her willingness to be angry and resentful in front of me. Whether I said yes or no, she had played her necessary role of rebelliousness.

The day after the November 15 demonstration, I thanked the girls for being so cooperative.

There had been violence the day before in the very place they would have been. But of course I didn't mention that.

The rebelliousness of youth isn't always in verbal protest. The hardest problems in the home, the school, and society in general are those where there is no obvious rebellion, where there is often the appearance of easy adjustment and even passivity—but underneath, in the subconscious, the resentment and the rage are slowly, slowly burning, until they erupt in some act that may seem totally unconnected with the submerged emotion, but isn't.

In the case of Anne, I did not translate some of her actions soon enough to prevent what happened.

Parents who never have time for their children—and they are no more numerous in one class than in another—suddenly are brought up short by a wholly unexpected acting-out of a long simmering resentment, coupled with a cry for love.

Anne is perhaps the ablest girl in the school. Her percentiles are 100. Her I.Q., 150. She is at MacDuffie because her small town school had no intellectual challenge for her.

She is a rather quiet girl, with a genuine interest in other people's troubles. The younger girls adore her. She is equally popular with her own group. She is a counselor and friend to everyone. Her voice is low, but the sympathy and sensitivity hang in the air as if they had weight. Brilliant, musical, artistic, kind—I have the feeling that she could run the school in my absence. I am very fond of her, and we have many talks. She loves MacDuffie and MacDuffie loves her.

She broke some minor rules, which I attributed to getting used to the school environment, but I was shocked the first time she broke a major rule: leaving the campus after dark. We had a long talk. I told her I'd have to put her on probation, and she said amiably that of course I had no other choice. She was very sorry to let me down. It was a good talk, and I felt very close to her. She knew that I felt she had done a very foolish thing, and she also knew that she was not "pegged." She had broken a major rule, but that did not mean that I considered her a rule breaker. I considered her a great kid, who happened in some foolish moment to break a rule.

Everything went on as before. I felt that Anne was one of the best girls in the school. I still feel it.

But the day came—and it was one of the saddest in my career—when she was discovered drinking, and I had to let her go. I'll never forget that afternoon.

Her parents were coming to get her at four. I talked to her right after lunch. I knew she had been crying, and I was hoping that my own emotions would let me get through the interview.

"Anne, dear, you know I don't want to let you go. You have done so much for the school, and for me. You have straightened out some of the girls, and you have just listened to others and made them feel better. In a few months, you have made a greater contribution to MacDuffie than most girls make in years. If there were any way I could keep you I would. You know that, don't you?"

"Yes, sir, I know. I know you have to do it. I wouldn't respect you or the school if you made an exception. But, sir, I love this school. It's hard for me to leave it."

"This school loves you, too. We don't want you to go."

The doorbell rang and the secretary told me the parents were waiting in the reception room.

"Go in and see them," I said, "and when you're finished I'll talk to them."

She went in. I could hear her mother crying.

Fifteen minutes later she came out. She seemed very calm. Almost pleased.

"I'll go up and get my suitcase," she said.

"If you have anything heavy, ask the housemother to get the caretakers."

"I don't need them. The trunk is already down." The girls were waiting for her in the hallway. I turned into the reception room to talk to the parents.

They were very understanding. Her mother was obviously upset but trying not to cry. I explained that it wasn't the end of the world. She could go back to the local high school, or, if they wanted a boarding school, I was sure I could get her into one, with my many contacts with headmasters.

"I'm sure you know," I said, "that you have a remarkable girl. She isn't any different after breaking this rule from the way she was before. All the fine qualities are still there. I like to think that good can come out of this situation; that Anne will realize that she has to think before she acts; that she has lost MacDuffie, not by being wicked but by being foolish. I'd love to keep her. I'm not afraid she'll do it again. I'd love not to punish her at all, but I have to tell the girls that there are some things we cannot accept at the school—and liquor is one of them. Anne understands."

"Yes, she does," her mother said. "She loves the school so much. I can't understand why she would do that. We have never been strict about drinking. She can have wine with us."

Her father spoke. "Why is it that our children get in trouble in school?"

"You have another child?" I asked.

"Yes, I do," he said. "My son was in difficulties at Andover last year. We must be doing something wrong."

And suddenly I could guess the story of Anne, and of her brother, too.

"Mr. Burt," I said, "do you mind if I make a guess?"

"Go ahead, I wish you would."

He was a handsome man, owner of a factory in upper New York state. He had graduated from Harvard and Harvard Business School. An attractive man, with a warm, attractive wife. A hard worker, I gathered.

"I may be wrong," I said, "but let me try. Anne is a very affectionate girl. Every adolescent girl needs a lot of loving, a lot of attention. Anne needs it to an unusual degree. Call it temperament, or what you will.

"My guess is that Anne particularly wants it from you. Adolescent girls tend to relate to their fathers—the first man in their lives. I know she admires you very much. I know she is proud of the success you have made; your appearance, if you'd let me say so; your easy manner.

"When Fathers' Day came, she told me she couldn't wait to show you off to the girls. She was desolate when you called up that you couldn't make it. I hope you made it clear to her how very disappointed you were."

He said nothing. His wife looked over at him. I went on.

"When a person keeps getting in trouble in an environment that she likes, she is often trying to say something—not to the people in that environment, but to someone else. Anne loves the school, and yet she behaves in a way that she knows can mean separation from it.

"Maybe, sir, she's trying to tell you something. Maybe inside, without knowing it, she's saying: 'Look, Daddy, notice me, please. I'm your daughter, and I'm fun to be with. I want you to notice me, to pay me some attention, to put your arms around me and tell me you think I'm wonderful. Wonderful, do you hear? Do you hear, Daddy? I know how busy you are, and how you have to be at the factory early and stay late, and problems you have with prices and all that, but, Daddy, I'm your daughter. Doesn't that make me more important than your factory, or your social life, or almost anything except of course Mother? Please, I'm sixteen, I'm growing up; I'm almost grown; and you don't even know I exist. Notice me, notice me, or I'll, I'll do something awful. I'll get pregnant, or I'll get expelled from school, or I'll take drugs and get arrested. NOTICE ME! NOTICE ME! OR I'LL MAKE YOU NOTICE ME SOMEHOW!' "

My voice had risen. The room was very still. Mrs. Burt was crying softly. . . . Her husband was looking past me at the wall.

He stood up and came toward me. "I guess I haven't been too good a father," he said. I pictured him back at his office the next morning, secure in the environment he understood best. I didn't know what had shaped him, either.

"Tell Anne we're ready to go." The voice was calm, controlled. I wished he would get angry. I wished he would scream at me that I was cruel and heartless for expelling his daughter. I wanted to hear him shout, or swear, or cry, but I knew that we would shake hands politely—as befitted men from the very best colleges.

I walked into the hall to say goodbye to Anne. She

wasn't there. I called up to the housemother. "Is Anne Burt up there?"

"No, she isn't," she answered. "She just went downstairs to say goodbye to you."

I went through the two front rooms and the hall, but I couldn't find her. I turned toward the door and saw a figure in the telephone booth. She had gathered up her hair from the back and pulled it over her face, so no one could see that she was crying.

I slid the door open.

"It's time to go, Anne," I said.

I held her for a brief moment. She shook her hair back from her face. Her eyes were red. We walked together down the hall and into the reception room.

"Here's your child," I said to her parents.

Her father extended his hand.

"Thank you very much," he said.

9 The Fourth R and the New Discipline

At the end of Chapter 7, when Susan came face to face with her real feelings about her mother, I wrote, "People talk about the 'real' world outside of school. It's a myth. If the real world wasn't there in the early morning for Susan, where was it?"

Education is the quest for the real world. The Fourth R is reality.

The best definition of education I know is the definition of mental health, attributed to Dr. Menninger: "The ability to deal constructively with reality." The definition applies equally well to education. In seven words.

Every word is important. *Deal* means that the student is active, not just sitting and absorbing. He is involved "expressively in his own education," to quote Benson Snyder of MIT. *Deal* implies that he has free will, B. F. Skinner to the contrary notwithstanding. The student by this definition is his own controller, not a "controllee" of patterning. How quickly the lines of controversy are beginning to draw around this seven-word definition.

The ability to deal "constructively" implies that there

is a right way and a wrong way to deal with reality, a good way and a bad way. The controversy deepens. Dr. Menninger seems to be implying that educaton is moral as well as intellectual. There is a whiff of a value system here, and many modern educators are scared to death to talk about values, lest they appear to have taken a moral stand—or "stance," to be very up to date. They are like the salesman in a toy shop, who was explaining an involved mechanical toy to the mother of a four-year-old.

"It seems awfully complicated for him," the mother said.

"Look, lady," the salesman replied. "This is an educational toy designed to prepare the child for life in today's world. Any way he puts it together is wrong."

But the bitterest battle in the world of ideas today centers around "reality." A funny thing happens on the way to the Fourth R—reality teaching. A great many brilliant, literate, verbal, and vocal psychologists, journalists, educators, and even clergyman stop you and say: "Look, fellow, there's no such thing as reality. It's all relative, depending on the street where you live. You don't teach young people reality, or content, or truth, or whatever you want to call it. Who are you to decide what is real and what is fantasy? You teach the young attitudes." You neither educate them, says Douglas Heath, nor do you "promote their self-fulfillment." You merely further their "educability," to use his favorite word. You teach them what the author of *Future Shock* calls "copeability," which he defines as the ability to "adapt to continual change" with speed and economy.

Well, attitudes may be important, but they are not enough. Listen to lover boy telephoning his girl with an old popular song on his mind:

> I would climb the snow capp'd mountains,
> Sail the mighty ocean wide,

I could cross the burning desert,
If I had you by my side. . . .[1]

"I'll be over tonight if it doesn't rain."

I have no quarrel with "educability" or "copeability" as parts of a program, but they are far from the center of reality education.

We can teach teachability, and educate for educability, and tell our students how to cope with copeability; but eventually the subject is confronted with an object, and something called reality education takes place. You can be forever alerted to the possibility of interpersonal relations, but the time should come when you find a friend you can trust or a girl in your arms.

So far in this book we have tried to show the needs of young people that are not usually stressed in discussions about them: the need to be important to the older generation; to meet the expectations of the adult world; to be sacrificial and courageous rather than demanding and spoiled; to be listened to with the insight and understanding of the Third Ear; and to have their words and actions interpreted in terms of the roles they must play as adolescents before they find their true identity.

The two generations have been talking together. They are now ready to explore the meaning of discipline and the part it plays in reality education. The burden is on the adult, as it should be.

The End of Father-Mother Bear and Father-Mother Sheep

Most people cannot make up their minds about discipline, any more than the dictionary can. The dictionary, of

---

[1] From "If I Had You," by Ted Shapiro, Jimmy Campbell, and Reg. Connelly. Copyright © 1928, renewed 1956 Robbins Music Corporation, New York, N.Y. Used by permission.

course, mirrors the confusion of the populace, as it is supposed to do.

As everyone knows, discipline comes from the Latin word *disciplina*, which means both "teaching" and "learning." Gradually, the idea of misbehavior and subsequent punishment became paramount in the minds of most people. The dictionary tries to ride both horses. On the one hand, discipline is defined as "training that corrects, molds, or perfects the mental faculties or moral character," and on the other it is defined as "punishment" and as "control gained by enforcing obedience or order." "To train or develop"—"to punish or penalize." We're a long way from an understanding of discipline.

There is no question how young people interpret the word. In our Sunday night get-togethers I have often asked students to describe what the word means to them. The answers are overwhelmingly similar: "Discipline is what happens when you have broken some rule"; "discipline is what the school expects of you in the way of behavior"; "to be disciplined is to be punished"; "if you're well disciplined, it means you have learned to do what you're told"; "discipline is being stern"; "when your parents are angry they will probably discipline you"; "discipline is what the older generation thinks the younger generation needs."

The overtones are familiar, and not confined to young people. How many times have you heard an oldster growl, "What these kids need is discipline." By discipline he means someone to get tough with them; put them in their place, wherever that is; tell them where to get off. The Father-Mother Bear approach.

Discipline is tough handling; discipline is letting them know who's boss; discipline is telling them to cut their hair or take a bath.

It is usually Father Bear who, on being defied for the first time, comes screaming to Mother Bear, "Why don't

you teach these children some discipline?" as he storms out
of the room.

But Father Bear is dead. He drowned in a torrent of
criticism from the very latest psychologists condemning
the "authoritarian personality"—and there is no doubt
that he had it. He did not know how to handle the youth
revolution of the sixties, nor was he helped by the schools
and colleges to which he had sent his children. He had an
idea that he had something important to say, but he didn't
know how to say it. He was lacking in humor, flexibility,
patience, and understanding. He used the wrong words at
the wrong time, and he shouted too much. He never quite
understood the difference between "authoritative" and
"authoritarian," and he was no student of trends.

He had come up the hard way, and the arrogance of
the affluent young jarred him. He lacked what anybody
who deals with young people especially needs: the ability
to put himself in their place. But he had standards, and he
expressed his convictions. He may not have been subtle,
but he had a certain impact.

He was unduly proud of not being a psychologist,
never realizing that what he was really proclaiming was
his ignorance of human motivation. He never thought of
adolescents as young adults, but waved the banner of
dependent childhood over anyone who wasn't "of age," and
lived and died believing that the older generation, and especially himself, could get the results they wanted to get
by putting their foot down, telling them off, and all the
rest of the clichés by which Father Bear lived in the days
of his glory.

However, he did have two areas of strength that made
him at least more attractive than his fiddle-faddling suc-
cessor, Father Sheep. He had convictions, and the young
admire people who have them—whether they share them
or not. Also, he sensed that power could not be delegated:
that someone has to be in charge and accept the ultimate

responsibility. But his view of power was limited and negative. He thought it was to direct people instead of to change them. He thought it was to prevent people from doing things instead of to give them the power to be strong in themselves.

Father-Mother Sheep read all the books, listened to all the experts, and ended up believing that their children must be so superior to their parents that the best that the latter could do was to cave in, give them what they wanted, and hope that they would turn out to be as "creative" and "self-disciplined" as the experts said they already were.

Whether he was a college president, bewildered by the appearance of some of his students walking out of a college dorm with guns in their hands in front of the TV cameras of the nation, or whether he was haranguing the faculty not to adopt punitive measures that might not be acceptable to lawbreakers, or whether he was an upper middle income slob whose children told him he was a dupe of the capitalist system for making the money that they were spending for him—Father Sheep never changed. He was determined to say nothing or do nothing that might sound critical of any young person. To paraphrase Sartre in *The Flies*, he intoned with endless abasement:

> Forgive us for living,
> For you are young.

When Father and Mother Sheep came to me in sorrow to tell me in broken voices that their daughter was on drugs, or had left college to become a ski bum, or was pregnant, I suffered with them, and for them. One does not tell them that they made mistakes. One tries to make them realize that nothing irreparable has happened, that the end of their daughter's life is not at hand, that the young have decades to live, and that they must live with them, and love them, and help them stand again. And one is ashamed at the category in which he placed two well-meaning, tragic figures who are weeping in front of him.

But their daughter is a tragic figure too.

We do not need a middle-of-the-road theory of discipline, halfway between Father-Mother Bear and Father-Mother Sheep. You cannot add the authoritarian and the permissive, divide by two, and come up with the best of both points of view.

It is precisely the points of view that are wrong. We need a whole new concept of discipline, a new method, a new goal.

I have not failed in the past to decry the pretentious word "new" when applied to some educational theory fished five decades later from the turgid waters of John Dewey's prose. Certainly, I do not pretend that no one has ever used the individual components of the discipline I am describing as "new." In dealing with adolescent boys and girls in college preparatory schools, I began to discover certain ways of handling even the most difficult disciplinary situations that produced results so different from the usual ones that gradually, inductively, I found myself developing a set of beliefs, assumptions, and methods that are a far cry from either "traditional" or "progressive" discipline. Nor are they a compromise between them. Hence, I am bold to call the results "new."

As the title of this chapter indicates, the Fourth R is reality, and discipline is an important aspect of reality education. Our central concept goes back to the original meaning of discipline as teaching. Discipline is meant to illuminate the real world and teach a person to live in it with understanding, confidence, and conviction.

We have to differentiate between the immediate disciplinary situation and the pervasive disciplinary philosophy and method that create a certain atmosphere in the community—be it a home or a school.

To the young especially, discipline comes into operation only when there has been an infraction of some rule, or a question of right or wrong behavior. They think of discipline as something that happens and then is over; i.e., the disciplinary situation and the ensuing penalty. Although discipline deals with behavior, it goes far deeper than the kind of behavior parents mean when they say, "Behave yourself." Discipline may involve punishment, but to equate the two is like saying that the purpose of pointing out mistakes on a French exam is to give a low grade. In other words, discipline is more than the disciplinary situation. It is not something that is dragged into the open for special occasions but a vital principle which permeates the every-minute living of the younger and the older generations.

It is this latter point, that discipline goes on all the time, whether in the home or the school, that often escapes parents and certainly students. When parents say that the discipline of the school is "lax" or "strict" ("firm" if they approve of it), they are vaguely aware that discipline is an ongoing process, part of the philosophy and atmosphere of the school, and that it is more than the sum total of disciplinary situations. However, they still may not realize that everyone is disciplined in a community. I have had parents tell me "Mary has never had to be disciplined," by which of course they mean that she has not been involved in a disciplinary situation, or punished for an infraction of the rules. But she has been disciplined nonetheless —whether she realizes it or not.

Major Assumption

Discipline is teaching, and the primary goal of every disciplinary situation is to teach. The lessons are infinite: that acts have consequences (the optimistic young find this hard to believe); that a good motive is not enough in either adolescence or adulthood; that one's rights are limited by the rights of others; that it is wrong to lower another's self-respect; that it is not true that in cheating you cheat only yourself, since you are actually destroying the fabric of honesty in the community for others as well as for yourself—a fabric that you will need when you want for yourself the fruits of other people's honesty; that the end does not justify the means, but the means often distort and deform the desired end; that you cannot be a parasite on the virtues of the community which have meaning and value to you unless you contribute to those virtues; that you cannot ask to be trusted unless you are trustworthy, since trust is a two-way street; etc., etc.

But the teacher has obligations, too. I say to parents and teachers alike: "In the disciplinary situation you are a teacher. You are bound to make judgments, but you are not a judge. You are not there to relieve your anger or show the muscle of your authority. Nor are you there to sermonize on the damage done to the school's good name. *The school is standing in front of you.*"

I have made mistakes when I was overly concerned about what people would think of the school, instead of what I could do to teach a girl her obligations to the school community. The two are quite different.

The equivalent in the home is: "Well, you have certainly disgraced your family and made your parents a laughingstock to their friends. I can't imagine what people will think of you doing a thing like that."

If there is real affection between parent and teenager (and that is the priceless ingredient in the teaching situation that we call discipline), the young person wants to know, not what damage she has done to the reputation of the school or the family, but what damage she has done to the feeling of respect or approval that the parent or teacher has had for her. (I do not mention love because the parent can never withhold love, regardless of what the child does, but love can wear an indignant face, temporarily.)

If her inmost thoughts were verbalized at the moment when the adult is angrily reminding her of the damage her behavior has done to the school's or the parent's good name, she would be saying (and I don't care how sophisticated or hardboiled she may appear): "I don't care what people will think of the school, or what your neighbors will think of you as parents. What do you think of *me*, not of what I have done? Do you still respect me? Like me? Love me?"

I am not denigrating the desire of any headmaster to have a school whose "image" is one of which he can be proud; nor am I criticizing the parent who is concerned both for her children's reputation and her own reputation as a parent. Everyone seeks approval from some person and some group of persons, in spite of the denials of professional "individuals." However, in adolescence the intensity of the search for approval precludes its being focused on more than a few individuals, especially of the older generation.

The teaching process can bring out gradually an awareness of larger and larger communities to which one has an obligation; but in a disciplinary situation the community is narrowed, for the adolescent, to a few key persons whose good opinion of her is part of her search for security, approval, and affection. As she comes to realize from the skilled and affectionate teacher and parent that she has not been permanently banned from their "golden opinion" of her, she is open to the implications of her action in the larger community. But not before.

Discipline is an adult and adolescent (young adult) discussing critical issues of right and wrong, and their implications. The teacher has not been successful unless the "you ought" that she is trying to explain is answered by a corresponding "I ought" from the student or child. It may take hours to get this reaction, and occasionally the student will withhold it lest he appear to have been "taken in" by the older generation. But that doesn't mean that the "I ought" isn't there.

10 Discipline and the Generation Gap

Is the Generation Gap a Myth?

Before I have a chance to close my ears to the angry screams of the authoritarians at that question, I have got to shake off the sticky-sweet embraces of the legions of youth adorers who are strangling me with advance approval.

The former cling to the concept because to disbelieve it would give them no leverage in parading their superior wisdom, experience, and lifestyle before their huddled inferiors, the young. The youth adorers of the Father-Mother Sheep variety disbelieve in the generation gap for all the wrong reasons. They think of youth as a cosmetic that they can regain by association with young people. To talk about a generation "gap" is to admit that one is no longer young, attractive, and exciting. On this basis, to discipline one's peers becomes an act of betrayal. One can only sit at their feet or by their side in the temple of eternal springtime.

They are upset when the churlish young tell them to "grow up."

Growing up is what the younger and older generation have in common. It is a lifelong process. Of course there is a gap in age and experience. And of course any member of the younger generation who preferred to be with her elders rather than with her own peer group would be in need of psychological counseling.

But this is a difference in degree rather than in kind. When I say I question the generation gap, I am talking about that concept of the generation gap that maintains that there are two societies in our culture, the young and the old, those under twenty-one and those over—comfortably over!; that the two societies are historically in opposition, with different goals, ideals, and values; and that the health of the country depends on the younger generation becoming the older generation as soon as possible. To those in the younger generation who inhale this last statement, the younger generation should become the older generation as soon as possible in order to take power and set the world straight; to the older generation of true believers, the young should become older as soon as possible so that their elders can set *them* straight.

Both of these hard-nosed groups forget that the teacher and the taught must meet on common ground if any learning is to take place, whether we're talking about discipline or academics. To enlarge the common ground is to decrease the generation gap.

Neither the authoritarian nor the permissive parent is close to her children in disciplinary situations. The Father-Mother Bear type becomes the judge, sitting in court over the accused, with all the panoply of power. The permissive parent merely denies the existence of the situation, or passes it off with a lazy "don't-do-it-again, dear."

Both of these postures outrage the adolescent, if only the parents knew it. It is an insult to one's dignity as a person and one's maturity as a young adult to be presided over by Judge Papa, who is no saint himself. Especially when Judge Papa is going to retreat from reasoned argument, judicial and serious in tone, to outraged denunciations of what he wouldn't have thought of doing when he was a young man. And for father or mother to deny that what son or daughter does is morally important is to place the adolescent on the same level as a child who is too young to be charged with responsibility for running naked into a crowded living room.

If a parent has to choose, and he doesn't, it is better to denounce than to ignore. A denunciation shows emotion and underscores belief. It is expressing the importance of a moral act—be it a matter of dishonesty, cruelty, or sex. To be excluded from discussions of right or wrong, and from any kind of emotional or intellectual reaction to the expression of either, is to be ruled a child who is not yet mature enough for moral considerations.

I was talking to a freshman, when I was a college Visitor of the Year once. The Visitor of the Year came down to the campus for four days, addressed the student body on any subject he wished, met with various groups and officers, and set up an office for anyone who wanted to talk to him.

The girl was talking about her boyfriend but was actually saying very little that was important.

Finally, I said: "You didn't make an appointment to tell me that your friend is blond, is a junior in college, and wants to be a businessman. Was there something specific you wanted to discuss, or am I guessing wrong?"

"Well, there was something specific but I don't know how to say it, or what you can do about it."

"I'm sure there's nothing I can do about it, but why don't you tell me anyway. It might make you feel better."

"Well, I'm sleeping with him," she said.

"And it troubles you, I gather."

She nodded and went on to describe the relationship that had begun when she was a sophomore at high school.

"We went steady for four years in high school," she said. "I didn't go with anyone else and he never dated any other girl. Will you tell me," she demanded indignantly with rising voice, "why my parents never even suspected anything like this could happen? Together all the time for four, now nearly five years, never going with anyone else. What's the matter with them, anyway? I knew it was going to happen. I knew I'd be upset about it. I wanted them to warn me; I wanted to talk to them about it; I wanted to ask them what to do, and whether it was a good idea to get started. But all the time they kept telling me what a nice boy he was, and I felt like screaming, 'What's the matter with you, anyway! Would you think he was a nice boy if you knew we were doing it? Am I a nice girl? What do you think we're doing when we're alone in the house? Why don't you wake up?' "

My mind went back to all the parents who lost their nerve as their children grew up. They did not want to argue with them; they dreaded the scenes that came when they tried to say no; they did not feel a match for them mentally; they did not want to "impose" their own beliefs on them; they decided that they really had nothing to offer except privileges. They listened to the experts—and they abdicated without meaning or wanting to.

Their children would somehow come out all right without their guidance. What they forgot is that someone else would be guiding them, whether they did or not. We are all guided by the people we are closest to *emotionally* and *verbally*. The people who talk to us become the people who love us. The people who fix our breakfasts, send us off to school, do our errands, pay for our clothes, send us on vacations, put us through college, and buy us a car or lend us theirs are different from the people we rap with, go out with, smoke with, and talk with for hours—about our feelings, our hopes, our fears, our beliefs, our problems, and something called "life," which we expect to encounter after school is over.

We have shut off our children without meaning to. We have kept them at a distance because we thought that was what they wanted us to do. They have formed their own circle of supporters from their own age group, the tightest band of young people in our history. The walls are all down. There is no geography, only the closed-in world of brotherhood. And love. And sex.

"I wanted them to wake up and talk to me," the little freshman said.

We'd better do it. We'd better step out of the double world of youth and age, and into the single one of people, some younger, some older, some less experienced, some more experienced. If we can reject the straitjacketed myths of the generation gap, we can accept further propositions about adolescents.

The Disciplinary Discussion

There are certain beliefs about young people and the way they should be handled that underlie the disciplinary discussion, the most important teaching part of the disciplinary process.

1. *Teenagers are young, sometimes very young, adults, who should be treated with respect and affection.* Of course, treating young people with respect does not mean kowtowing to them or letting them run all over you. It does not mean putting them on Boards of Trustees or letting them take over the home, the high school, or the college. It does not mean that we must never criticize them or get angry with them. Anger can be more a sign of respect for them than unearned and vague approval or that chirping sentimentality that makes them far more perfect than they are—or want to be, as I shall discuss later.

2. *Adolescents and adults basically want the same kind*

of home, school, or world and believe in the same goals.
"Basically" is the key word here. The question may be
asked, "If they want the same kind of home, or world, why
is there such conflict between the two groups?"

The answer is the same as it would be for almost any
problem in our society, or in our personal lives: Why do
people who marry in rapture divorce in bitterness? Everyone wants a warm and lasting personal relationship. They
don't fight over the goal. They fight over the *means* to that
goal.

The male chauvinist feels that a happy marriage is
one that permits him the kind of dominance he associates
with men-women relationships. If his wife is not a masoch-
ist, she will feel that a happy marriage is achieved in other
ways. The conflict is inevitable.

Everyone wants to be loved by others, but throws
away that goal by using the wrong means: sarcasm (see
how clever I am); arrogance (see how important I am);
ill temper (see what a strong-minded person I am: I don't
take anything from anybody); etc.

Misguided means to a mutually desired end are the
agents of our personal conflicts. Adult-adolescent relationships are no exception. The parent or teacher who has
never questioned his own mistaken means to a desired end
will not be able to help a young person change his.

The two generations are closer than they think, in
spite of differences in actions and *stated* beliefs. The willingness of young people to let everyone do his own thing
does not apply to their parents when involved in extra-
marital affairs, nor do teenagers believe in ripping-off when
their own money is stolen, vandalism when their possessions are trashed, or cheating when someone is dishonest
with them.

3. *What sometimes look like irreconcilable differences are
merely the necessary questioning and the role playing of*

young people (a role playing that is encouraged by the generation gap concept I have criticized). See Chapter 8.

4. In the disciplinary discussion, we have the oportunity to gain the *assent* of the teenager to the fairness of the discipline, including the punishment; and, still more important, to the truth of what we are trying to teach her. *Assent* is a key word.

5. *The adolescent must not feel that she has been "pegged" for whatever she has done to bring about the disciplinary situation.* On the grounds that our opinion of her *is* important to her (as hers is to us), we never tell a young person she is dishonest, or a troublemaker, or a liar. We tell her that she has done a dishonest thing but that we have confidence (we'd better) in her fundamental honesty; that she has made trouble but we consider her basically a cooperative person; that she has not told the truth but we do not look upon her as a liar; that we *do not punish her* (*if punishment is indicated*) *because we are afraid that otherwise she will do the same thing again,* but because—well, let's leave that to the chapter on the meaning and purpose of punishment.

What we are saying here is crucial. We just do not believe that teenage actions, no matter how deplorable and wrong (why be scared of that word?), express that finality of mental and moral cast that we call character. We are in work with adolescents for that very reason.

We believe, and we let them know we believe, that we do not accept their actions as expressing their real selves, and that no matter what we feel we may have to do in serious disciplinary situations right up to expulsion (of course there is no "expulsion" from the home), we have lasting confidence in them—and we love them.

Does it work? Nothing else does.

6. From No. 5, it is immediately obvious that at the end of the disciplinary process and the accompanying penalty,

the student is immediately restored to the trust and affection of the parent or counselor. Parent and adolescent start all over again. It is as if nothing had happened. Whatever was done is over; the discussion has followed and the implications have been pointed out; the penalty (if any) has been given. As far as the counselor or parent goes, the record is *completely* clear again. It is important that the teenager know this, and she is only going to know it if she is told. She has to be told in more than words; i.e., she has to feel it in her bones and not only in her head. The ability of young people to sense what an adult really thinks and feels, as opposed to what he says he feels, is uncanny.

Parents, especially, find it hard to reprimand, discuss, punish—and forget. The offending offspring is always around to remind you of what he did last week; and his father has to hear the story all over again when he comes home from work. In my counseling with parents, I suggest that one conference with both parents, if the matter is sufficiently important, is preferable to two parents individually going over the other's arguments again. And then— restoration and silence. It takes self-control, but the dividends are immense.

7. Our philosophy of punishment will be discussed in succeeding chapters, but the subject, naturally, has already come up in presenting specific disciplinary discussions. One cannot isolate the factors involved in the disciplinary situation until each has been thoroughly explained. The reader should already know by now that *punishment is the least important part of the disciplinary situation* and the *disciplinary discussion,* with its emphasis on teaching, is the most important part. But punishment does have certain uses, to be discussed later.

8. We *always* believe a girl unless we have *proof* that she is lying. We *never* say, "Are you sure you didn't do this?" To ask her whether she is involved is itself a kind of promise to believe what she says. You are not telling her she

did it—you don't have proof—you are asking her. To question her answer "No" is very obviously to distrust her. If she is telling the truth, and you doubt her, you have lost her forever. If she is lying (as she may very well be), you have at least a chance to win her over. You are giving her credit for being more truthful than she is. Let her boast about fooling you if she wants to. The burden is still on her, not you. If she feels bad that you trusted her and she lied, you may help her become truthful. If she is proud of lying to you and considers you a fool for believing her, your chances are much smaller, but you still have a chance.

You don't start out by asking her whether or not she did whatever it was, especially if the penalty may be unpleasant. You don't want to lock her in with a quick lie that she will be embarrassed to change later on. You tell her exactly what evidence you have that *seems* to involve her, and you emphasize the "seems." You tell her that you are going to ask her in a few minutes wehther or not she was the person (or one of them) involved, but you ask her not to answer until you have finished talking.

You explain that if she says no to the question asked, that will be the end of it: you will take her word for it. You tell her *exactly* what the penalty will be if she says yes, even if it is expulsion. You tell her that you can't change the penalty because she admits her fault, much as you would like to. And you tell her why, as I shall do in an actual conversation. But you also tell her that if she tells the truth, and the truth is "Yes, I did it," the truth telling is more important than any penalty you could give her. And it is.

She knows by now that *she* is going to make the decision, with no pressure from you. If she says, "I didn't do it," she is believed, and she is free. If she says, "I did it," she will suffer consequences—but you will respect and admire her.

Shall she lie and go free, or tell the truth and be

punished? And how much will your admiration for her weigh against her parents' anger and disappointment? She could lie this once and then never lie again, couldn't she? And look at the girls who had lied and gotten away with it. . . .

She is going to have to make a very difficult moral decision. Isn't that what growing up is all about? What right have we got to keep her from it in order to avoid a painful decision of our own?

Mona

Mona's story involves many though not all of the eight items of belief that underscore our philosophy of discipline.

Mona is a new girl, with a strong personality and a will of her own. Her father is dead, and her mother, an alumna, is finding it difficult to bring up three children alone.

Mona is unresponsive to dormitory regulations—to put it gently—and is in a more or less continual battle with her house director. I have spoken to her several times with no visible effect.

On this particular morning, she is in my office for a more serious breach of rules which could mean a one-week suspension. There is strong evidence against her but not what I would call proof. So, after going over the situation for several minutes, along with the penalty if she says that she did it (I never liked the phrase "guilty of the offense," which sounds like a criminal before a judge), I tell her:

"Mona, although there is some evidence in your direction, there is certainly no proof. If you say you are innocent, that is the end of it. I'm delighted to believe you. If you say that you did it, I'll have to suspend you for a week; but I want you to know that I shall admire your courage in confessing when you don't have to, and I'll let your mother know that I think you're a great person and that she should be proud of you for telling the truth when it hurt—which is much more important than what you did. Now which is it?"

(It is important not to sound as if you had made a decision in your own mind as to what the answer should be. "I'm delighted to believe you" should sound as if you meant it, and you *should* mean it. Your private misgivings aren't important when you are establishing a trust relationship between you and the young person.)

She looked at me with cold hostility.

"I didn't do it," she said aggressively. "Why does everyone always pick on me?"

"I don't think anyone has picked on you," I said, not too pleasantly. "I asked you a question, and you answered no. I couldn't be more pleased. Run along."

Almost five months later, still getting into difficulties with almost everyone in authority, she knocked at my door.

"Sir, may I see you?"

"Sure, come in, Mona. What's on your mind?"

"Do you remember in October when I told you I hadn't done anything wrong?"

"Yes, I do. I was very pleased."

"Well, I want you to know I lied. I did it."

"I'm still more pleased, not that you lied but that you told me the truth when you didn't have to. That's good news. You and I can start now on a whole new basis. We can completely trust each other. That's a lot more important than what you did. I'd like to ask you one question. Why did you decide to tell me this five months later when you know you were home safe?"

"That's what bugs me," she said flatly. "I can't imagine why I should come in and tell you something like this. It's not a bit like me," she added hopefully, as if she had contracted a strange disease which she would try to throw off the next time it attacked her.

I smiled. "I think you're nicer than you try to make out."

"Don't kid yourself, sir," she said, "I'm not nice at all. This is a funny place. It's hard to lie at MacDuffie."

"I like to hear it," I said. "I find it hard to lie here, too."

"You!" she said in astonishment. "Why should you want to lie?"

"Why not? I'm no different from anybody else,"

"But you're the headmaster!" she exclaimed, as if headmasters had been granted a special dispensation from lying. She could just as easily have said, "my mother" or "my father." They want to be able to admire adults—us.

"You make me sound like a pious dope," I told her. "Headmasters are no better than anyone else in what they want to do." I emphasized the "want."

"Why don't you do whatever you want to do?" she asked.

"You might think less of me."

"You mean just me?"

"You—and everyone else. Let me explain. You can expect certain things from me and I from you. If I get up in chapel and talk about telling the truth, you don't expect me to lie. And even if I don't discuss it in some talk, you have a picture in your mind of what a teacher, a headmaster, a parent should be like. We hope it's a good picture, and we don't want to let you down. Maybe we helped make the picture. We don't want to blur it. But we have a picture of you, too: of a straightforward, honest person, whom we can trust and believe. Now that you've told me the truth, the picture is clear, and I like what I see. It took courage to tell me when you knew you'd be suspended for a week. That's another part of the picture. And you didn't really want to get away with something that other people have been punished for. You wanted to take your medicine, too. Do you see why I'm pleased?"

"I think so. But I didn't sit down and figure all those things out. When do I leave?" she asked abruptly.

The quick change of subject, which I have experienced many times, is characteristic of young people in a conversation that gets a little too close to their deeper emotions. Contrary to popular opinion, young people do not show their real emotions easily. They are too self-conscious, too much afraid of being laughed at. They are more likely to make fun of their emotions than to express them, to cover them up rather than to expose them. They will express their emotions freely and intimately (and with utmost sincerity) about social injustice at home and abroad, but the farther away it is from their own emotional life, the more vocal it is likely to be.

I have seen this tendency in very simple situations. Just before Christmas vacation students gather around a log fire to sing carols. When we move into the more emotional melodies, "I'm Dreaming of a White Christmas," "Silent Night," and the mood around the fireplace deepens with the expectation of seeing their families and of renewing at least in memory the symbols of the religion of their believing childhood, the last notes of "Silent Night" give way, almost invariably, to "Jingle Bells, Jingle Bells"— sung at the top of their young voices, sometimes almost shouted, as if to repudiate any impression that they had been moved by the more emotional songs.

So, when Mona abruptly changed the subject by asking when she would leave, she was really saying: "Don't talk to me any more about trust and truth and how pleased you are that I confessed. I want to think it all over by myself. I don't want to agree with you too quickly. I don't want to be conned by an adult."

This desire to be left alone and allowed to sort out in her own mind whatever she has heard should be respected. The assent that we want from the young must come from within. We cannot and should not try to hurry the process.

"I don't want you to leave," I said, "until I've had a chance to talk to your mother. And I don't want you to talk to her until I have. OK?"

"OK."

"Why don't you wait outside."

I called up her mother, the kind of call I have made many times: "Mrs. Doyle, this is Ralph Rutenber. Your child is well, so don't be worried. We have a disciplinary situation here that I think actually is a good situation as it has turned out, even though I'll have to punish Mona."

I went on to tell her the story of the original denial and then the confession.

"What I want to stress is the fact that this happened almost five months ago. I believed Mona because we prefer to believe young people—and we are not afraid to be fooled. There was no reason for her to come to me and confess, except her desire to be trustworthy when she was trusted. I want you to be happy about it. I want you to feel that a turn has been made in Mona's way of thinking: The school is getting to her. When you come to get her, I want you to throw your arms around her and tell her how proud you are that she told the truth—when it hurt."

"Do you have to send her home? After all, she told you of her own accord. I'm afraid that the punishment will make her sullen and angry again."

"I don't think so. She knew she would be punished when she confessed. It's only for a week, and I won't let it affect anything important."

"Does she know she'll be suspended?"

"She knew it before she admitted that she had lied. Mrs. Doyle, if I tell the students that if they confess, they'll get out of the penalty, or have it lessened, I make it too easy to confess. I tell the students at the beginning of the year—so often that they won't forget it—that I cannot reward them for telling the truth; that I want them to tell the truth because that is the only way this community, and society itself, can survive. However, I also tell them that although I cannot make a difference in the penalty, their telling the truth when it really hurts and when they don't have to, means that I shall not only have a very high opinion of them but that the punishment itself becomes unimportant; it is not given because they need it. It is given, as most punishments should be given to adolescents, because it says something—not only to the girl but to the community—about the real world. The world inside of her and the one outside.

"The punishment becomes the girl's contribution to the school, not a means to force her to be good. By telling the truth when she didn't have to, Mona said that she *wanted* to make that contribution. She wouldn't put it that way—it would sound awfully prissy and goody-goody. But that's what she means. She did something; she accepted, even asked for, the penalty. That erases the past and she starts all over again, with me, and with herself.

"I want to see her off before she goes, and I want to be at the door when she comes back on Saturday. Let me know the exact time. And please don't tell her how hard it is for you to send her here (she knows it); don't tell her you're disappointed (you shouldn't be); tell her you're proud of her for telling the truth, and tell her that with your arms around her."

"Thank you very much, Dr. Rutcnber. I'll be there tomorrow morning, and I'll drop in your office."

I wish I could say that Mona was a completely different girl after this experience, but it wouldn't be true. What is built slowly changes slowly. Mona continued to be difficult for both teachers and house parents to handle. She and I had a good relationship, and she knew I was very fond of her. However, she found it difficult to accept school rules when they interfered with what she wanted to do, although she was never in serious trouble again.

She came to see me in the spring of her junior year to tell me that she would not be back the next year.

"I feel very bad," I told her, and I did. "I've really

looked forward to having you march down the aisle on graduation day, and get your diploma from me. Why do you want to leave?"

"Can I belong to the Alumnae Association?"

"You certainly can, and I want you to. You still haven't told me why you're leaving and where you're going."

"It's hard to explain it, even to myself. I've tried harder to be good in this school than I ever have before, but I think you know it doesn't come easy. Sir, in spite of your faith in me, I have broken almost every major rule in the school, and I would be expelled if you knew about it. What do you think of that?"

"I don't want to know what you have done. Remember, I have a kind of contract with the students: No one has to confess anything at MacDuffie, unless she is specifically asked about a specific incident; and she is never asked unless we have some reason to believe that she was involved. I expect you to tell the truth when asked—you've heard this before."

She smiled, and I went on.

"You told the truth, however belatedly. I think you're great. I want you to stay. You know that if I hear about your other 'exploits,' I'll ask you, because I have to. And you'll tell me the truth, because we now have that kind of relationship. I'll take a chance on what I don't know, if you will."

"But I'm not sure I'll be any better this coming year, with senior privileges and all that, and I don't want to let you down."

"I appreciate that. I never want to let you down either. I'll take a chance if you will, on the past and the future."

Her voice was beginning to break. "Sir, please don't make it hard for me."

"I won't make it hard for you. I promise to put no more pressure on you to stay, as long as your mother approves. But don't decide it today. I'll hold a place open for you until the first of July. Let me know before that. And don't forget how much I wanted you to stay."

She said, "Thank you, sir," and almost ran from the room.

She wrote me in late June that she was going to a private day school near by. I keep the letter among my very special ones.

I didn't hear from her again until three years later, when she had finished her sophomore year at college. It was a phone call.

"Hello, sir. This is Mona."

"Well, hi! How are you? Where are you? And what are you doing?"

"I'm going to get married," she said, "and I wondered if you could perform the ceremony."

"Well, I'm very pleased and proud you want me, but I'm afraid your marriage wouldn't be legal. I'm not a clergyman."

"But aren't you something in the Episcopal Church? I thought perhaps that would cover the law."

"I'm what they call a lay reader, which means I can read the lesson; but that's all. I can't marry people—even you."

"I'm awfully disappointed. Will you and Mrs. Rutenber come?"

"You know we will if we possibly can. When is it?"

"We haven't set the date. We just decided to get married. Mother knows about it."

"Let me know when it is to be. I want to hear all about him some time, but I know this is a long distance call. How was your school, and how did college go?"

She told me the name of the college.

"Neither of them went at all well. I know it's my own fault for being such a rebel. I hope I have a good marriage. Do you think I will?"

"I'm sure you will."

"MacDuffie was my only good experience. I'm sorry I didn't finish."

"Don't have any regrets. You did what you thought best, and maybe it *was* best."

"Don't let the school ever change, sir."

"I won't. I promise."

"I'll let you know the date of the wedding."

"Fine. I'll see you. And thanks for asking me."

"Goodbye, sir."

"Goodbye."

She looked rather fragile as she walked down the aisle on her uncle's arm. I haven't heard from her since. I hope she has a good marriage.

11 Discipline: Actions and Implications

I have no statistics to prove it, but I believe that the great majority of my students have told me the truth when they could have lied and gotten away with it. Most of them told it at once, after I had talked to them first. The only thing different in Mona's case was the length of time it took her to decide, and her own obvious bewilderment as to why she was being so honest!

I have even had students tell the truth when they knew it would mean expulsion, and the letters they have sent me later are the most moving I have, and too personal to publish.

Why?

First, they were *expected* to tell the truth if asked. Second, although the expectation came from the administration, the peer group must have been one that supported the truth-trust idea. The fact that, even in the sixties, when young people were not only expected to oppose their elders but were enjoined to do so in the name of peer group solidarity and the fantasies of the pundits that moral wisdom was the peculiar property of young people, the number of students who told the truth and took their medicine did *not* decline. The generation gap is more contrived than real.

Since many people seem to be trumpeting the opposite view, both the youth adorers who believe that the young are the reincarnation of Moses, leading us begrimed adults to the promised land; and the youth haters, who prefer to believe that a great moral gap is fixed between those who have different ways of dress and of lifestyles—the conviction that the young and the old have essentially the same beliefs *has to be taught.* And the disciplinary teaching situation can give a personal and painful focus from which the two generations can explore this concept together.

Honesty

Take the question of honesty, in my opinion the major moral problem of our society. We read of adults teaching twelve-year-olds how to cheat in order to be national racing champions; of brilliant young scientists "fixing" their research to prove what they want to prove; of political figures right up to the very highest level lying, conniving, and perjuring themselves. People who seem to consider themselves honest cheat on their income taxes, smuggle unreported goods through the customs and brag about it, make false calls to announce they have arrived somewhere. Theft, which tends to sound more like a joke than a crime when it is called a rip-off, is at an all-time high; shoplifting is confined to no income or social class; cheating in schools and colleges is overwhelmingly prevalent; and construction men tell me that if they want to keep any tools from their own group, they have to be just a few feet from them. Why was anyone surprised at Watergate? How many *completely honest* people do you know?

More than drugs or liquor—and these are not small problems—the widespread belief that lying and cheating and even stealing, on a very small scale of course, are not serious character flaws, is undermining our society. I tell a parent that it is good for a student to be caught while she is still young. The trauma of being discovered, having to face her parents and, hopefully, the disciplinary discussion—with its implications—may turn her around before dishonesty becomes a way of life to her. Let's look at a cheating case.

She has finally confessed, although it is harder to get a student to confess cheating than almost anything else I can think of. The evidence of two almost identical answers was presented, and all I said was: "Either you or Gloria copied from the other. I took you first because you were first in the alphabet, and I like each girl to make her own decision in private. You know that we don't publicize discipline. So I'm asking you whether or not you copied this from Gloria on the exam. I don't want you to tell anything on Gloria. I'm talking to you, only about yourself."

She was very tense.

I said nothing about the fact that Gloria was an excellent student and she an average one. That would be weighing down the scales, perhaps giving her an excuse in her own mind, and worst of all piling mental failure on top of moral. Young people need as much success as possible —don't we all?—and a quick recovery from the sense of guilt, *but not so quick as to make them feel that they have done nothing wrong.* Besides, excellent students are as likely to cheat as mediocre ones. Rich men take bribes. Dishonesty, including theft, carries no label.

"I haven't said I did, but if I did cheat, would you have to tell my parents?"

I gave no indication that the question was revealing.

"I'm afraid I would. I would want a headmaster to tell me if my daughter cheated, so we could talk over the whole question of why people have to be honest; why they have no choice."

"A lot of kids cheat, both in public school and here."

"I know. A lot of adults cheat, too. Of course that doesn't make it right."

"Miss Johnson says that when you cheat you are only hurting yourself."

"Who is Miss Johnson?"

"She was my teacher in seventh grade."

"I'm afraid I don't agree with Miss Johnson."

"You don't?" She seemed surprised, as if she had never dreamed that anyone could disagree with Miss Johnson.

I wish the earnest Miss Johnsons of the world would stop telling their students that they are only hurting themselves when they cheat. It isn't true, but it is very comforting.

"We can talk about Miss Johnson before you go. You haven't told me whether or not you cheated on the test. Did you?"

"Yes, I did," she said in almost a whisper.

"I'm glad you told me the truth," I said. "I'm proud of you for saying yes. Let's talk about cheating."

"Are you going to tell my parents?" she asked in trepidation.

"We'll talk about that later," I answered. "I want you to listen to me for a few minutes. People can talk when they have leveled with each other. Now relax, and let's talk."

She didn't look relaxed, but I went ahead.

"It's no good for me to do anything about your cheating on the exam unless you agree with me that cheating is wrong. The question is what kind of school you want."

It was essentially the same kind of conversation I had had with Susan, when she forged her mother's name to a permission. I've had it many times.

"You want an honest school. I think you want the teacher to correct your paper, not just put a grade on it.

You don't want the school to cheat on its food. You want it to be good food. That's what you paid for. You don't want the school to tell you how excellent the teachers are and then have you find out that some of them can't teach at all well, and don't even know their subjects.

"You want to read the catalogue and when you come here find out that it was an honest catalogue that told the whole truth about the school.

"You want an honest world, don't you? You don't want to be shortchanged by the cashier at the movie, or pay for a pound of candy when it really only weighs three-quarters of a pound. You don't want anyone to give you a counterfeit ten-dollar bill.

"If you want an honest home, an honest school, an honest world, you've got to be honest. You have no options. You can't let others create a world that is honest for your benefit unless you contribute to that world by your own honesty; otherwise you're a parasite, aren't you?"

She answered with the sentence I have heard more often than any other one except, "Sir, may I see you?"

"I never thought of it that way," she said.

They want the same kind of world that we do: honest, trusting, fair-minded, compassionate, and loving. That isn't a soft world. That's the hardest world there is. Unbreakable.

I talked to her parents as I had talked to her. She was more than ready to accept the academic punishment involved. In fact, she wanted it. Four years later, if the college had asked whether or not she had ever been disciplined for dishonesty, I would have told them—in honesty—of this incident. I would have added my belief that it was a single incident and never repeated. And the college would have accepted her on my conviction. However, I wasn't asked that. I was asked, "Do you have complete confidence in her integrity?"

My answer was yes. And I did.

When I give lectures on the psychology of discipline and mention an incident like the above, I am often asked in the question period: "Suppose the student cheats again, when you have been thinking that she is honest. What do you do?"

Of course this happens, although not as often as people suppose. A disciplinary situation should have some element of arrest in it. The adult is saying to the young person: "Hey, wait a minute. What are you doing?" The disciplinary discussion should be pointed and specific. It should have an edge to it, but not an edge that permanently wounds. The young person, however, should remember it as an unhappy experience—as well as one where something was learned.

If the Father-Mother Bear approach is used, the adolescent is castigated, the adults are disappointed in her and very angry with her, and the punishment is barked out in high-wire indignation. It is a memorable experience, all right, and will have some preventive effect—chiefly the avoidance of being caught at it the next time.

If the Father-Mother Sheep technique is used, the parents or parent surrogates will whisper their sorrow, then smile indulgently and tell their child, as one of them told her daughter in my presence, "I know you didn't mean to cheat, Eleanor."

Eleanor looked pleasantly pensive, as if to say that she had opened her French book in a dream, and hardly knowing what she was doing found out the exact meaning of the word that had puzzled her.

I wasn't about to let it go.

"What your father means, I am sure, Eleanor, is that you didn't *plan* to cheat, that you came into the examination with no idea of cheating. I am happy to believe that, but I am sure we would all have to say that you know that reaching inside the desk for your book and opening it on your lap during the exam was cheating. Right?"

"Yes, sir."

To get back to the question of the person who cheats a second time, I certainly don't want to imply that the disciplinary discussion I am describing automatically produces an honest person forever after. It might cause the person who had never cheated before to stop cheating permanently. But if cheating has become a habit, one "arrest," so to speak, however painful, will not necessarily be a cure.

The point is that in this kind of discipline the factors of success are as favorable as the adult can make them. No more can be asked than that. The experience has been painful, and the penalty has been given.

However, the disciplinary discussion is much more pointed on the second occasion. We do not believe in cumulative punishment, i.e. making the second punishment more severe than the first. The student has already been punished for the first offense, and we told her that was the end of the incident. We can't go back on it. But we can ask searching, uncomfortable questions, and we can remind her that there has to come a time when *she* makes the decision to stop what she is doing. And the time is now.

"The Day of Small Things"

We have been talking about suspensions, expulsions, serious penalties for breaking rules. This is the kind of thing that many people mean by discipline.

However, if discipline is teaching, and if it permeates the everyday life of the school or home, it will inevitably deal with what are called "small things," or minor infractions. I use the phrase "so-called" because I am convinced that everyday discipline is, by definition, more important in building character than the dramatic, and sometimes traumatic, events that rack the community of home and school and society.

The argument that, in a world full of violence, drug addiction, theft and corruption in high places, the "little sins by which we live" are unimportant just isn't true.

There are two great moral heresies in our society: one, that the end justifies the means; and two, that only the "big" events that bring about discipline from the small community or the larger society are important. Most of the big events wouldn't exist if the small ones were taken care of seriously. The injunction to "despise not the day of small things" means that those "things" are not really small.

And yet our society is permeated with the indulgent fallacy that everyday disciplinary situations are not very important. Essentially this is the same argument that police often get from parents whose children have been caught throwing rocks through windows: "Why don't you go after real criminals instead of kids who have just broken a window or two?"

Maybe a broken window is a minor object, but there is nothing minor about the wanton destruction of property, or violence. Ask the shopkeepers who lost their livelihoods in the 1977 blackout in New York City. It is the job of the counselor to point out *the large implications of little acts.* No one knows when a person who tells lies becomes a liar; when a person who "swipes" a candy bar begins to take the money to buy one, or two, or something more expensive, or an automobile. No one knows whether or not anyone will necessarily graduate from what seems a trivial action to what is obviously a grave one. But there is a time, as every psychiatrist knows, when actions express the total character, the way the whole person reacts to temptation or crisis or desire of some kind—and the total character is not trivial.

We cannot get away from discipline as teaching— everyday teaching. We cannot get away from the importance of the relationship of the teacher to the taught, in discipline as in English, French, and woodwork. If in any teaching situation there is no bond of respect and, hopefully, of affection between student and teacher; if the teacher is convinced that the student is "dumb" and cannot learn, or the teacher has no confidence in his willingness to do so, very little significant teaching and learning will take place. The teacher described by Somerset Maugham in *Of Human Bondage,* who began his classes "in a rage" and ended them "in a fury," would hardly be the ideal teacher, no matter what his subject.

This does not mean that the adult in a disciplinary situation should never get angry. We are teaching reality, and young people have every right to learn that certain actions cause people to get angry. There would be something artificial—and a disciplinary situation is the very last place for the artificial and the contrived—in an adult, either parent or counselor, who was all syrup and sympathy when an adolescent has, let us say, grossly interfered with another person's rights.

But anger must be carefully handled, and I mean handled. Controlled but obvious anger, a reaction to an immediate discovery, can start the disciplinary interview, sometimes with good effect, depending on the personality of the student involved and on what she has done. But it cannot set the tone of the interview if any lesson is to be learned—except that the adult has the power, damn him! One cannot sit down for forty-five minutes and teach anything at the top of one's temper.

Even in a quick lesson of few words, anger should be brief. It should always be a beginning, if used at all, never a middle, and never, never, never an end—even of a one-minute situation.

I'm not going to say an "unimportant" situation because it lasts a minute. A good deal can be learned in sixty seconds, although much more in sixty minutes. But discipline goes on all the time, as I said before, and the cumulative effect of so-called "minor" disciplinary situations can sometimes prevent the major trauma that shakes the personality even while it is hopefully cleansing it.

So I have no apology to make for using unimportant

infractions to point out important implications. Implications are a vital part of all teaching.

No adolescent is going to go through this process by herself, whether the problem be academic or disciplinary. A girl does not call her parents after an algebra exam and gush: "Oh, Mother, I had the most wonderful time in the algebra examination. I analyzed problems, made distinctions, and came to conclusions. Unfortunately, my conclusions were wrong, but I did derive great satisfaction from the intellectual process."

Instead, she is going to run crying to the telephone and scream to her parents: "I flunked my algebra test cold. Get me out of this school!"

Just as she needs the parent or teacher in the academic situation to point out the implications of the algebra problem, and to remind her that a failing grade in a test is not the end of the world, she also needs the adult in the disciplinary situation to explain the implications of her action, and to help her understand that the penalty, if any, is not directed against her personally as revenge for a past error or blackmail against a future one. It is rather a way of teaching both her and the community to think before acting. The assent of the young person to the point of view of the adult, to the justice of the penalty, if there is one, plus her feeling that she is immediately restored to the confidence and affection of the adult once the situation has been explained, is the touchstone of success in the disciplinary teaching situation. It may take sixty seconds; it may take hours; and many parents and counselors are not willing to take the time that is necessary to bring out this agreement. But that is what it is all about. The rest is parsley.

Sixty-Second Discipline

Beverly is sneaking out of the dining room with four oranges concealed in paper napkins—nothing that is likely to bring her before the U.S. Supreme Court. The rule is: Eat all the fruit you want at the table, but don't carry more than one orange, banana, or apple to your room. We serve fruit two and sometimes three times a day, but we're not supplying you with it between meals.

Beverly runs right into the headmaster, coming in early for the second lunch shift.

Headmaster: How many oranges are you taking to your room?

Beverly: Four.

Headmaster (after a moment's silence): Why don't you become a member of the student body?

Beverly (confused): What was that, sir?

Headmaster (sharply): Why don't you become a member of the community and not try to get special privileges for yourself? Why wait till almost everyone has gone so you can get more oranges than anyone else? Why not join the human race and accept the restrictions that your fellow human beings live under?

Beverly (stiffly, and with a martyred look): I'll put them back.

Headmaster (who wants assent): You don't think you ought to, I gather. If you don't think you ought to, keep them.

The tone is still sharp. The headmaster starts to go.

Beverly: Sir, I'll put them back. I'm sorry.

Headmaster (smiling): You're a nice person. Thanks a lot.

Beverly puts them back—stuffed with virtue. We both smile as she leaves the dining room.

Trivial? I don't think so. What's trivial about special privilege? What's trivial about grabbing for more than your share?

She wasn't called a "selfish girl," but the questions asked implied a selfish act. The two are very different.

Assumption No. 5 in our kind of discipline maintains that the girl must never be made to feel that she is a selfish girl, a dishonest girl, a troublemaker, but an essentially unselfish girl who has done a selfish thing, an honest girl who has yielded to the temptation to be dishonest, a co-operative girl who has been making trouble.

In the brief incident above, "You're a nice person. Thanks," is an expression of your confidence in the kind of person she is, or may become—not in the kind of selfish person she seemed to be. "Thanks" is what it implies: appreciation for changing her point of view. The sharp tone of anger has been replaced by a certainty that you and she see alike. She is restored to your good opinion, not pegged as a greedy person. If you have any kind of relationship, she values your good opinion. And you value hers.

Minor discipline—yes. But not trivial.

Sixty-Minute Discipline

"Sir, may we see you?"

"Sure. Come on in. What's on your mind?"

"The house director told us to see you. We didn't go to the concert tonight. We stayed in the dormitory instead."

A group from a neighboring boys' school was giving a band concert. In courtesy to them, I wanted the whole student body there. I had told the girls several days before to get their studying done, as I would expect them to attend the concert. The two girls had stayed alone in one of the dormitories when the rest of the girls had been at the concert with the teachers and housemothers—hardly a world-shaking crime! Knowing the girls as conscientious students and good citizens, I also knew that the act was not one of defiance, but probably a desire to study. But there were implications to the action, and I wanted to point them out. *Implication* is a big word in the kind of discipline teaching I am talking about.

"You knew that you were supposed to go to the concert?"

"Yes, sir, but we have a French test tomorrow, and we wanted to study for it."

"Did you sign out to go?"

"Yes, we did."

"You signed your own names? Nobody signed for you?"

"No, sir."

They knew I would not have asked for the name of the other girl if another girl had been involved. At the high school age, the peer group is too close to be expected to "tattle" on one another. Only an unusually strong adolescent can "take" the inward guilt of being responsible for the punishment of one of her own contemporaries. Still harder to accept would be the merciless psychological beating she would take from her fellow students as a rat fink. One does not have to approve of the code to accept its validity for young people of a certain age at a time in history when the peer group is a more solid phalanx than the Roman military square.

"Are you the only two girls taking this exam?"

"Why, no, sir, of course not." The tone was one of surprise.

"In other words, about fifty French II students are taking this exam?"

"Yes, sir."

"Did you all get together and decide to cut the concert?"

"Oh no. It was our own decision. I don't know of anyone else who is cutting."

"Would it be fair to say that you figured that most girls would go on to the assembly?"

"I guess so."

"In other words, you assumed that practically all of the students, including those taking the French II test or any other, would go on to the concert in accordance with their signatures—promises, you might call them—and that would make it unlikely that you would be caught.

Whereas if everyone who had an exam tomorrow, or just needed an extra hour to study, stayed home, it would certainly be very risky for *anyone* to stay home. Right?"

"We didn't think of it that way. We just wanted an extra hour of study."

"I realize that you didn't sit down and analyze it, as I have, but I do think that those ideas, perhaps unconsciously, were in your mind.

"What you really said to your fellow students, whether you realized it or not, was: 'You simple slobs are going to play the game, sign up, and go to the concert the way good little citizens are supposed to. That will give us a chance to stay home, without being caught probably, and have one more hour to study than you'll have.' "

There was dead silence.

"In other words," I continued, "you hid behind the skirts of the other girls to get an advantage over them. I don't think that ought to make you feel very pleased with yourselves."

"We're sorry, sir."

"I know you are"—and I did, but I wasn't quite finished.

"I do want, however," I said, "to carry this along a little farther if you don't mind. I'm not trying to make you feel worse. I'm not trying to pile it on. I just want you to try to see this incident differently from the way you did.

"When you signed your name that you were going to the entertainment, you really made a promise. You said, in effect, each of you, my signature is my bond, my character, my integrity, my honesty. I promise you I'm going to the concert.

"You also said a few things about the honor system by your action. You said, and I don't mean that you meant to say it, that it was naive of the school to expect students in this day and age to do what they're supposed to do, unless you check them out. I want to ask you about that, and I want you to answer with complete honesty.

"Do you think we should check the dormitories before a concert, and also check you in and out of assembly with lists?"

"Sir, you know we don't." The distress was evident, and I wanted to get the discussion over with, as soon as possible. But I wanted to make my point.

"How would you feel if we did?"

"We'd be burned up."

I smiled. "I know you would! I can hear the indignant voices—all over the school. 'He's going to check us in and out of every assembly—like children. The housemothers are going to search the dorm rooms to' be sure we've all gone. And this is supposed to be a school that trusts the students!' "

I raised my voice in indignation, and the girls smiled.

"I think we can all hear the sound and fury," I said, "but you can't have it both ways. Nor can anyone else. Do you want a school where you're trusted?"

The answer was emphatic, "Yes, sir!"

I knew they were sorry. I wanted to restore their self-respect.

"I know you girls didn't think of all those things. You made a mistake, and I've pointed out all the implications. The incident is over, and we start all over again together. I'll have to give you some penalty, but you don't need it for yourselves. It's your contribution to the community. I really hate to give you any. What shall I do with you?"

One of the girls had said very little, but she spoke up now: "We'll be glad to take any penalty you suggest."

"Why don't you campus yourselves for a week—and thank you."

"Thank you, sir."

Big implications—from a small action.

Lynne

The case of Lynne could be called minor discipline, since the only penalty was to be a stiff bawling out. But is it ever minor to hurt a person's feelings and lower her self-respect?

Lynne was a vivacious, attractive girl, who did not like to be "bossed around," as she told me once. The boss in this case was the dormitory prefect, who checked out the students' rooms every morning. The prefect was firm and conscientious, Lynne's room was almost invariably messy, and the conflict between them grew.

Lynne had her own coterie of prefect haters, who lost no opportunity to make Marilyn, the prefect, look as ridiculous and as overbearing as possible to the other girls in the house. Marilyn was aware of their enmity but stuck to her guns and did her job, with as much opposition from Lynne and her group as they dared to show without getting into trouble with me.

Just before the junior prom, Lynne was given a wholly unexpected weapon against Marilyn. The latter had asked a certain boy to come to the prom. He had refused, explaining that he would be away at the time; but Lynne asked him, and he accepted. And Lynne knew that he had turned Marilyn down. She made the most of it.

I was unaware of the whole matter until Marilyn came to my office, greatly agitated. She was such a strong girl, so capable and confident, that I was unprepared to have her burst into tears and tell me: "Sir, I want to resign as prefect. I just can't take it any more."

I waited for her to stop crying. It took several long minutes.

"What's the trouble?" I asked her finally.

"I'm the laughingstock of the dorm," she sobbed. "Lynne has never liked me, and she is going around and telling everyone that Hank Wooster turned me down for the prom and is going to go with her. Her friends give a

big laugh just after I pass them in the hall; and I know
what they're laughing about. They grin when I ask them
to do something. They say, 'Yes, Marilyn, whatever you
say,' in a smirky voice. When I opened the door this morning, there was a note pinned on it: 'What's the matter,
Marilyn? Can't you hold your man?' "

She burst into tears again,

"I can't take it. I can't take it. I want to resign. I
want to get out of that dorm. Please, sir, please!"

"Don't cry," I said. "There must be a solution to this.
Why don't you talk to Lynne privately about this?"

"I can't, I can't," she wailed. "You talk to her."

She was more defeated than I realized.

"Marilyn," I said, "if I talk to her, she will know you
told on her, and you will be persecuted all the more. You
know you always look so much on top of things that they
probably don't think you're bothered at all. I am sure you
could swing it yourself."

"I can't swing anything," she said. "I'm completely
licked."

It's a phrase I hate to hear from anyone.

"Don't give in to this feeling," I said. "I want you to
sleep on this and come back to me tomorrow."

She came back the next day, and I knew from her face
what the answer was going to be. She was just barely in
control of her emotions. I wondered how much she had
slept.

"I've thought it over," she said, her voice quavering,
"I don't feel I can handle it. You talk to Lynne, please. I
can't be any worse off than I am."

Cruelty, whether mental or physical, has always upset me a great deal. After Marilyn left, my anger against
Lynne and her friends began to rise. I decided to give
Lynne the bawling out of her life: to point out what she
was doing to another person, for no reason other than the
fact that Marilyn was trying to do the job to which she had

been appointed, with the approving votes of her fellow students. I would let her know how spiteful and cruel it was of her to twit Marilyn about the boy whom Lynne had persuaded to come to the prom.

Furthermore, I would let her know specifically that girls like her were not what we were looking for at MacDuffie, and if she and her parents didn't like what I said they could come down and take her home. Tomorrow!

In that frame of mind I called the dormitory where she lived and told the housemother, "Send Lynne up to my office at once." From my tone of voice anyone would know what was going to happen to Lynne.

Fortunately, the dorm was the most distant one from the office and, while waiting for Lynne, I began to realize that this was not the way I told parents in PTAs and clubs to handle their adolescent sons and daughters. I was throwing away all of the advice I gave others to remember that discipline was teaching, and that the adult should ask himself what was the best way to get the young person to agree with his point of view. There are times, especially when one is full of righteous indignation, when it is hard to practice what one preaches so smoothly and effectively when the emotions are at rest. An expert on discipline is a man whose children have gone to bed.

By the time Lynne arrived, I was in control of my emotions and knew what I was going to say to her. She came in with a half-defiant, half-scared look, as if she knew what was coming.

"Sit down, Lynne," I said quietly.

She sat down and leaned forward a little. Her hands moved back and forth over the arms of the chair.

"Relax," I said in a low voice, "I'm not going to scold you or punish you for anything."

She looked surprised and confused, as if she didn't know what was coming next.

"As an actual fact," I said, "I really should congratulate you, although I'm not doing so. Some people would,

because there is no question that you have done an outstanding job in doing what you set out to do."

She looked down at her hands.

"From what I gather, you set out to cut down another
person; make everyone laugh at her; humiliate her; cause
her to lose her pride and self-respect; and show her and the
whole school that you could get a boy who had turned her
down.

"I just want to tell you that you have succeeded completely. She is really crushed. She has lost her self-confidence and her self-respect. You have won—hands down.
She was in here yesterday crying and saying she wanted
to quit her job as prefect."

Lynne looked up in amazement. "Marilyn," she said,
"crying?"—as if she couldn't believe it.

"Why, yes," I said, "Marilyn. Isn't that what you and
your friends wanted? Isn't that a kind of ultimate tri-
umph? Shouldn't you feel happy about it?"

She didn't say anything.

"That's all," I said. "I just wanted to tell you. Run
along."

She walked out slowly.

The next morning Marilyn came rushing into my office.

"Sir," she said, "you'll never believe it. Lynne came
into my room last night and apologized for trying to get
my goat! She said she had no idea I would take it so hard.
We're going to be friends. Do you understand? Everything
is going to be all right in the dorm. I am so glad I didn't go
through with my plan to resign. That was a narrow escape,
wasn't it?" she exclaimed.

I didn't tell her that it was I who had the narrow
escape.

Aftermath

The week before school was out, when girls were sitting
on the campus benches among the trees and the moon-
light, and the seniors were realizing that they would not

walk the paths again as undergraduates, my car was parked at about 9:30 outside my office.

As I went out to get in and go home, I found that Lynne was sitting on the porch steps.

"Sir, may I talk to you for a few minutes?" she asked.

"Sure," I answered, "why don't you get in the front seat, and we'll talk there. It's cooler out here than in my office and just as private."

We took our places, and she began.

"I'm sure you know I'm not the gushy type, but in the last few weeks I've come to a few conclusions, and I want to tell you about them. I've suddenly realized that I have gotten a great deal from this school, but I haven't given anything to it. It's been all take, but no give. I want to do something for it, but there are only six days left. What can I do? How can I make it up?"

"Lynne, what you can do is give more of yourself to your next community, and to whatever community you go into after college. If you've learned something here, you have all your life to practice it, so everything you do for other people will be an extension of MacDuffie. What more can we ask for? I don't agree that you have given nothing to the school. You contributed a great deal when you apologized to Marilyn and changed the whole spirit in the dorm. And I suspect there are other things that I don't know about."

"There certainly are," she said emphatically, "and I don't plan to tell you about them, either."

We both laughed.

12 The Many Faces of Punishment

There are many questions we have to ask about punishment. It is not a simple concept or procedure. What are the purposes of punishment? What are we trying to teach by it? What about the deterrent factor? "Computer punishment"? The community effect?

The person who is in a position to inflict punishment has to ask himself searching questions. Did the young person assent to the justice of the punishment? Did she keep her self-respect and my confidence in her? Did I say what I wanted to say to the community, without verbalizing? Did the student consider the punishment her contribution to society or retribution from it? This last question is one that has been consistently overlooked in discussions of punishment.

In the *Home Book of Shakespeare Quotations*, the subtitles under "Punishment" are "Beating," "Condemnations," "Correction," "Retribution," "Threat," "Torture." Even the most ferocious Father Bear could hardly find more than two categories here for his fifteen-year-old daughter or son, and Father Sheep is already halfway up the street in flight. As usual, we shall get no help from either group, and God knows little insight, either.

In the first half of this century, there was a widespread belief, based on a misreading of Freud, that, if you denounced anything, you secretly yearned for it. If you expressed indignation over an act of cruelty, you would be accused by some pseudopsychologist of harboring a secret desire to be sadistic. To be indignant over a sexual assault was, aha, to be exposing one's own unconscious prurience. Professional youth lovers hammered into our collective sense of guilt the idea that the adult world was somehow responsible for any act of dishonesty, cruelty, or violence on the part of young people. No wonder that we stand unnerved in our hair shirts, dripping with guilt, at the prospect of punishing a young person.

Even if the adult world were wholly responsible for the actions of teenagers, it would not be good for the teenagers themselves to believe it. We may feel that a young person has committed theft because of a lack of parental love and poor home conditions, but it is better for *us* to consider him a victim of society than for *him* to do so. Otherwise, he has a perpetual excuse for taking other people's property. "I am a victim of society. I came from a sordid home background. You will therefore understand why I feel impelled to rob you."

As Action sings in the *West Side Story*, when the Jets gang has run into Sergeant Krupke, the policeman:

> Dear kindly Sergeant Krupke,
> You gotta understand—
> It's just our bringin' upke
> That gets us out of hand.
> Our mothers all are junkies,
> Our fathers all are drunks.
> (All)
> Golly Moses—natcherly we're punks!

And again,

> (Action, to A-Rab)
> My father is a bastard,
> My ma's an S.O.B.
> My grandpa's always plastered,
> My grandma pushes tea.
> My sister wears a mustache,
> My brother wears a dress.
> Goodness gracious, that's why I'm a mess![1]

The Purpose of Punishment

We have to see punishment in terms of the teaching of reality, and we have to remember that all of us are part of a community and do not exist *in vacuo*. The community is real, too.

One purpose of punishment is to teach that acts have consequences, both to the actor and to the community. No young person will ever learn this truth if he or she is never punished.

I'm talking about the discipline of adolescents, not criminal actions. The punishments I'm talking about do no permanent harm to the young person. If properly handled, and preceded by the disciplinary discussion, they teach him an important lesson in the world of reality: that to do wrong carries a price tag to the actor, along with an obligation to the community to repair its breached fabric of honesty, truthfulness, and trust. This idea of contribution to the community is not a high-flown, "spiritual" concept but a practical down-to-earth procedure. More of it later.

I am using the word "wrong" in the broadest possible sense. At the bottom of the scale are small acts of selfishness, insensitivity, and unwillingness to accept the obliga-

---

[1] From *West Side Story,* by Arthur Laurents and Stephen Sondheim. Copyright © 1957 by Leonard Bernstein and Stephen Sondheim. Reprinted by permisson of Random House, Inc.

tions of the community while still demanding for oneself its rewards. I am talking about *acts* of selfishness and insensitivity, not selfishness and insensitivity as fixed elements in the character. Young people have not yet developed the set character of adulthood. Acts of selfishness, if "arrested," discussed, and atoned for in the disciplinary situation, may diminish until the person becomes either less selfish or, hopefully, unselfish.

Insensitive remarks that hurt another human being may be pointed out, as Lynne's were, in order to prevent the girl from becoming an insensitive person.

At the top of the scale are acts that involve moral wrong, such as dishonesty, serious infringements on the rights of other people to live full and happy lives, and wanton destruction of the property of others.

The kinds of punishments I'm talking about also involve a wide range. The penalty may be only the sharp voice of the adults, as in the case of Beverly; it may be left to the conscience of the teenager, as in the case of Lynne; it may be a temporarily tough bawling out, followed by the disciplinary discussion and, as with *all* punishment, the restoration of the young person to the affection and respect of the adult. It may be a temporary or permanent separation from the school community. This last penalty can be used in the school—never in the home.

Computer Punishment

Mechanical systems of punishment, of the action-reaction type, I call "computer punishment." Computer punishment teaches no lesson except that the adult world has the power to make you uncomfortable for what you have done. Maybe the student decides that whatever he did was more than worth what he paid for it. (Maybe a few years in prison is worth the million dollars that you got dishonestly.)

In school, it is often the detention system: Late for class—one detention; late twice in a week—three detentions; forgetting lunch duty—extra duty for four days. I am not decrying specific punishments for specific things. Guidelines for the student are necessary. I am merely saying that no teaching is involved if that is all there is to it: if you do certain things, certain things happen. Persons who are always late are acting selfishly. They inconvenience other people. They may be acting with quiet defiance. "You say to be here at six o'clock for dinner, but I'm going to take my own sweet time." People who do not do their share of work are freeloaders and parasites on the working community, and time should be taken to point it out to them. The disciplinary discussion.

I have sat in the room of the assistant headmaster of a large boys' school, while boys filed into the room with slips of paper from teachers and houseparents describing their sins. The interview was as long as it took the disciplinary officer to read the slip; sometimes a few seconds, at most half a minute.

"Disturbance in class—three extra study halls. Report to Mr. Martin."

"Failures to do make-up work during Christmas vacation—stay one day over for Spring holidays."

"Keeping the dormitory awake at night—loss of next .overnight."

It reminded me of one of the jingles of my childhood:

> One, two, three, four, five, six, seven;
> All good children go to heaven.
> When they get there they will yell,
> All bad children go to hell!

Report to Mr. Martin. . . .

Punishment as Deterrent

Punishment teaches the lesson that acts have consequences, but *it does not teach the lessons of right and wrong.* It is at this very point that our type of discipline diverges sharply from the Father-Mother Bear belief that treating them rough will make them good little girls and boys, and from the Father-Mother Sheep idea that they are already such good little girls and boys that they shouldn't be punished at all if they say they are sorry.

The real teaching part of the disciplinary situation is not the punishment but the *disciplinary discussion* between adult and adolescent, as I have already illustrated in my stories. To learn that acts have consequences is not necessarily to learn that they are wrong. It may be only to learn that they are inexpedient, unwise, likely to be found out.

From parents, from school, from experience actual or vicarious, including the experience of discipline, young people internalize ideas until they become a part of them —their character. You cannot build a character out of expediency. It involves no ethics, only a knee-jerk reaction to be careful.

On the other hand, there is no reason to belittle actual punishment or the fear of punishment as a deterrent to wrong action. It is true that deterrence is hardly the ideal basis for morality. In deterrence, of course, the motivation is external. What unpleasant thing will happen to me if I do this again—or for the first time? The question does not involve the ethical self or awareness of the rights of others. However, if the reckless driver becomes more careful because he once lost his license—whether he *believes* in being careful or not—he is less likely to injure himself and some other person. We would prefer for him to be careful because he values human life, including his own, but we won't quibble when he drives past us instead of into us.

A recent study of honesty on the campus indicates very clearly that talking about honesty, discussing the reasons for it, and trying to make it part of the value system of young people did not actually stop the cheating that was going on until it was pointed out that the students would be punished the next time.

So punishment can be a deterrent, both for the individual involved and for the community at large. But it is more than that.

Punishment as Reenforcement

Besides teaching that acts have consequences and acting as a deterrent, punishment reenforces the really important lesson about right and wrong that is hopefully learned in the disciplinary discussion.

Let me give an analogy from my own profession. I was an English teacher before becoming a headmaster and for a short time afterward. All teachers come face to face with the dilemma of grades. There are teachers to whom grades are retribution. "You did poorly on your theme. Here's your failing grade." Black ink—red pencil. "You did this —I'll do this." But the purpose of writing compositions or themes, as we call them—is to learn to write.

At the same time that you give the student a low grade on a composition, you must bolster his confidence that he can do better. To try to increase his confidence by pointing out only the good parts of his composition, glossing over his errors, and giving him a grade that does not represent the quality of his writing and thinking is dishonest. To say that grades are in themselves punitive and should be omitted is to prepare the young person for a world where he and his work will never be evaluated— which means a world that does not exist.

The encouraging comments that you make about the composition—and I used to tell my English teachers always to find something to praise in every paper—are not enough if you fail to point out the weaknesses. However, if you merely point out the weaknesses in a pleasant conference in your room, he will nod his acquiescence, admit his errors, thank you for going over the paper with him, and, one or two weeks later, when he sits down to write another composition, he is likely to remember euphorically the praise but not the criticism. If you give him a failing grade on the paper, he will remember that; and you will reenforce the fact that he needs to write with greater care.

The same thing happens in the disciplinary discussion. One of the excitements of working with young people is that they are frank enough to tell you what they really think. When a student in the disciplinary discussion admits that her action was wrong, at least nine times out of ten she means it. Her position cannot be compared to the sophisticated adults of Watergate, who were "shocked" at their own behavior—after it was exposed. The young person's character is not set, and her experience is limited. She is almost always genuinely sorry.

To the extent that the girl is mature and reliable, the adult who is involved in the disciplinary situation is quite right in feeling that she will not do the same thing again. I have told many young people that I would like to let them out of the penalty because I was convinced that they did not need it for themselves as a reminder, but I did not let them out.

Our faith in young people must be realistic. Young people will flee as from the plague the sentimentalist who approaches them with warm doe's eyes and sticky fingers to do them good. They want only to deal with adults who know their fears, their limitations, and their weaknesses —and love them anyway.

Realistically, I must be aware how easy it is to admit wrong sincerely, and genuinely regret it during the affectionate intimacy of the disciplinary discussion; and how much more difficult it will be to fend off temptation six months later alone, on an examination perhaps, when the year's work is at stake.

The student may need that extra remembrance of

punishment to reenforce his new intentions to be honest. But even if he doesn't need this reenforcement for himself —and no one really knows—the *community* needs it vicariously in several important ways.

Punishment and the Community

Every act that involves punishment obviously tells the community, as well as the individual, that acts have consequences. But punishment does more than that. It teaches the community—and I'm still talking about teenagers— the gradations of punishment; i.e., the degree of importance that society puts on one action as opposed to another. Hopefully it causes the members of the community —especially if it is small and personal, as in the home and in many schools—to think more specifically about problems of right and wrong, the relation between the individual and the community, and the relation between the peer group and adult society. Even if the punishment is indignantly decried by the peer group, it still may force them to fall back on their thinking processes—and that's what we want them to do, isn't it?

The fact that every penalty says something to the community at large is the answer to the question: Why punish a person if she is sorry for her action and you are sure that she will not repeat it?

We must bring our young people face to face with reality. If we teach them now, we are preparing them for the future. In the world of adulthood, you cannot say to the court of law that you are sorry and won't do it again. If you drive carelessly and hit someone, you will be sorry all your life for it; but you will still be punished for manslaughter, or driving to endanger if the person survives.

I try to explain to my students that I can't let them out of the penalty, however much I would like to.

I tell my students that I cannot say to the community, "If a girl admits she was wrong and feels bad about it, no punishment will be given." To say that to one girl is to say it to every girl in the school, and to say it to every girl in the school is to invite damage and even destruction to the community. It would mean that anyone who, in the opinion of the headmaster, seemed sorry about any act would not be punished. How does one distinguish between the girl who is genuinely sorry and the girl who is faking it in order to get out of a penalty? How can he say to one girl, "I know that you're sorry, so nothing will happen," while he says to another, "You may be weeping, but I have decided you are just upset about being caught and are not really sorry. Therefore, you will be punished." It would be chaos if punishment depended on one's subjective evaluation of whether a person's regret was genuine or not. It would be playing God with a vengeance.

I have to say to the community, "Certain actions bring certain consequences." The distinction that I can and do make between the motives of different people, the kind of people they are, my subjective evaluation of whether the act really represented their total approach to the school or not, should be *expressed directly to the student.*

We need to realize that every wrong act weakens the fragile architecture of the good community. I read in the newspaper some time ago that in Omaha, Nebraska, "a crowd shouted and cheered as a gunman robbed the concession stand at the City Auditorium of an undetermined amount of money." There were forty or fifty persons in the group "around the refreshment stand Saturday night when a man produced a gun and demanded money. They (police) said the crowd watched the robbing and cheered as the suspect fled."

No one in that crowd would have cheered if he had been at the receiving end of the robbery. To applaud the man who, on threat of murder, takes money that someone else has earned is a wholly disheartening reminder that a group of strangers have somehow lived in communities which fostered a disregard for a man's right to earn and keep his bread without putting his life on the line.

The sum total of the beliefs and actions of a community, be it a home, a school, a neighborhood, a city, or a nation creates an atmosphere almost palpable, in which either good or evil are in the ascendant. In Hitler's Germany, the so-called good, certainly respectable, church-going middle-class could watch without comment or apparent concern while a Jewish professor was dragged up the streets by a gang of toughs, or while the Jews were beaten up on the streets by Hitler's storm troopers. The piling up of violence, buttressed by savage oratory, eventually deadened the compassionate conscience of a supposedly Christian nation.

So, every dishonest action creates an atmosphere which makes it easier for more dishonest actions to follow and more difficult for people who are trying to remain honest to do so—especially if they are young. In the days when racial jokes were acceptable at almost every level of society, people who wouldn't think of making those jokes today were making them, and people who didn't laugh were considered stuffy.

Every infraction of community standards makes it easier for someone else to further weaken the fabric of the community. If then the person is genuinely sorry for whatever he did and really believes in the standards the community has set, his punishment—and the way in which he accepts it—is a contribution to the restoration of those standards rather than their continued erosion.

The Desire for Punishment

The willingness of healthy adolescents to accept punishment and even at times to *want* it appears to have eluded not only their parents but the wide array of experts who write about youth. I say "healthy" adolescents to differentiate the willingness to accept punishment from the neurotic need to be punished which we call masochism.

Mona in Chapter 10 certainly wanted to be punished or she would not have admitted that she had lied about what she had done. In Chapter 11, the girl who cheated and the two girls whose minor infraction carried so many community implications wanted to be punished. "We'll be glad to take any penalty you suggest," one of them said.

I could give instances where I have said to a boy or a girl, after a thorough disciplinary discussion, "What penalty do you think I should give you?" Almost invariably, the penalty they set is more severe than the one I had in mind and actually gave them. They are not trying to win brownie points. They do not tell me earnestly, "I want to make a contribution to the community." Young people don't talk in any such self-conscious and priggish fashion, nor do they think in those terms. But consciously or unconsciously— and what difference does it make which it is?—a great many teenagers who have either been brought up to be ethically sensitive to the community or have learned suddenly in a disciplinary situation their obligations to the people around them actually want to be punished and square themselves with society—however they may define the word.

One of the troubles with our present theories about punishment is that we think of it only in terms of an individual situation between parent and child, teacher and student. If we talk about someone "paying his debt to society," we are not thinking of our own children. We are thinking of people who have committed murder and other major crimes and have gone to prison for them.

Let me give an example.

When I was a master and coach in a boys' school, I had bawled Ken out for some infraction I have forgotten and told him he could not go to the movies that night. He came in to see me after football practice.

"Sir, you told me I could not go to the movies tonight."

"That's right."

"Well, sir, I don't think that's a fair penalty." The adjective irritated me.

"Well, sit down. Why do you think it isn't fair?"

"We don't get to the movies very often, and I think you should let me go and figure out some other penalty."

"What would you suggest?"

"You might campus me for three days."

"If I campus you, how can you get to the movies? That's what I'm doing—for tonight."

"I mean campus me after tonight, beginning tomorrow morning."

"In other words, you want me to campus you when you weren't planning to leave campus anyway. Right?"

"But we don't get to the movies much in this school, and I think it's not a fair punishment."

Again, I winced at the "fair," but concealed my dislike of the word.

"You knew there were movies tonight, didn't you?"

"Yes, I did."

"But you went ahead anyway and broke the rules. Why should I wait until tomorrow to punish you?"

He was getting surly.

"Because we never get to the movies much in this school. That's what I'm telling you."

"I know what you're telling me. You're telling me that whenever a penalty is inconvenient or hurts a bit, you want it postponed to some time when it won't bother you at all. Suppose I gave you a week's campus and there was a very desirable activity on the day when your campus was over. Would you think it was fair if I delayed the campusing a day so that you would be sure to suffer a bit? Wouldn't you say in *that* case that the penalty should start when the infraction was discovered?"

"Yes, I would—but since we go so seldom to the movies, I think you should make an exception in this case."

"There's no such thing as an 'exception' for Ken Sherman. If I make an exception for you, I make it for everybody. In other words, I have a new rule. And that rule says that, if you're not willing to take your punishment like a man, I'll soften it for you."

He was stung. "I didn't say that," he exclaimed angrily.

"That's what you've been saying all afternoon. You just don't like the way I'm wording it. Let me tell you something. I'm going to let you out of it. I'm not going to sit here all afternoon and have you cry-baby the penalty. If you don't think it's a fair punishment, go ahead and go to the movies. There will be no further punishment. Now beat it."

My tone was sharp. He looked upset.

"Well, I'm not so crazy to go," he said.

"I want you to go," I snapped. "I don't want you to miss that movie."

"Well, I may decide not to go at all."

"Look, Ken," I said emphatically. "I want you to go to the movies. That's an order! That's what I'm letting you out for!"

"I don't wanna go to the movies," he wailed. "Please don't make me go."

Of course I didn't make him go. This approach could easily backfire. You have to take a chance on your judgment of the kind of person the boy is. I figured that, in spite of the whining attempt to get out of the penalty, he would react to the challenge of being able to "take" it, of being a man, of sharing the community lot.

When I got to a girls' school, I suddenly realized that there was no feminine equivalent for the phrase, "Be a man." But I think we're getting to it.

What About Previous Behavior, Extenuating Circumstances, Exceptions?

These problems are more difficult in the school than in the home. Parents who function in the tiny and very intimate community of the home are answerable only to the other children—usually one or two—and their own sense of consistency. However, they must still move very carefully in these three areas, especially that of previous behavior, to be sure that they do not punish the difficult child more severely than the one who is agreeable and cooperative.

In the school, the situation is more complex because the community is so much larger. In both home and school, the limits should be clear and the penalty for serious offenses explicit. Young people want to know where they stand.

Since the sixties there has been a tendency to avoid unpleasant situations by stating, as in some independent school handbooks, "The use or possession of alcohol or drugs is strictly forbidden and may result in dismissal." The key word, of course, is "may." The student is not stupid and realizes that this is no hard and fast regulation, but a statement half threat, half cop-out.

So Johnny Jones is caught drinking, let us say, and he is expelled. Johnny Jones has been a difficult boy to handle, aggressive, unpleasant, uncooperative. He has been suspected of taking drugs but nothing has been proved. He has previously been punished for insubordination and general hell raising. He is not the ideal citizen of Unrest Hall.

On the other hand, Jim Merriwell has been a pillar of the school, president of his class, a fine basketball player, a boy with an engaging personality and as popular with the faculty as with the students. A hard worker in his studies, too. Six months after Johnny Jones has been sent home, Jim Merriwell has been caught drinking, to the utter amazement and dismay of the administration.

If you expel them both, you are saying to the rest of the students in the school that this particular institution will not permit drinking. Everyone will understand it, whether or not they approve of the regulation. But if you remember that weasel word "may," you are in trouble. You are likely to find yourself saying to an outraged community of young people: "Anyone in this school who drinks will be dismissed unless he is President of the Senior Class, or holds some other position of influence or authority that bespeaks his school spirit."

Previous behavior in my opinion cannot be made the basis of *penalty* or lack of it for any specific action. There is certainly a point where a person who shows consistent refusal to abide by the regulations of a school community may be told that he may not return the next year. In the broad sense that could be called a punishment, but it is not a penalty for a specific deed. If a person has committed punishable actions in the past, they have supposedly been punished after the disciplinary discussion. Once the penalty has been given, in our form of discipline, *the matter is over* and the young person is returned to the respect and the affection of the adult. To give him a different penalty for the next action because of his "previous record," so to speak, is to put him in double jeopardy.

The reverse is also true. If four people commit a punishable act and one of them has had a clean disciplinary record in the past, the punishment should be the same. But it should be explained to the student, as I have done many times:

"I don't believe what you did expresses your real self. I think you were carried away by the excitement of the moment and didn't want to be 'chicken.' I wish I could make a distinction in the penalty, but I am sure you will understand that I can't do it. I have to say—never in words, of course, but by what I do—that certain acts carry certain penalties. I don't think you would really want to get out of that penalty. But I do want you to know that I make a distinction in my mind between girls who may do the same thing but carry a very different set of values. I feel very good about you. I think you're an asset to Mac-Duffie. I want to have girls like you in the school, but when you do step out of line I have to give you the same punishment as students who I feel—and hope I'm wrong—have less sensitivity to the school and less real concern for what it stands for than you do. OK?"

The answer is always an echoing and appreciative OK.

And how do we make these distinctions about "extenuating circumstances" without making the student feel she is not really responsible for what she does, or making the community feel that punishment depends on adventitious factors?

Do we try to discover whose "idea" it was and give him the heavier penalty? How do we know who is telling the truth if both accuse the other? Do we decide who is the more sophisticated and give him a more severe penalty because he "seduced," so to speak, a more innocent person into an action that was punishable?

Do we get into problems of amount? If you only took a few swallows of liquor or smoked one-half of a marijuana cigarette, are you punished half as much as the person who drank double your amount or smoked a complete joint?

If you stole a sweater but admitted it when questioned, are you less of a shoplifter because you told the truth, or only less of a liar than your partner who denied it? And if you get out of the penalty, or have it lessened because you admitted the truth, have you learned anything more than a procedure to avoid a severe penalty?

I am of course aware that the criminal law system permits plea bargaining, immunity, and other exceptions. A great many Americans have objected to such "deals" as were made in the Agnew and the Watergate cases, but this really has nothing to do with what I am saying. We are talking about teenagers who are being disciplined by people who love them. I maintain that in the community environment of a school, young people's previous exemplary behavior, their motivation, and their contribution should be expressly appreciated in the disciplinary discussion in a way that makes them aware that you do not consider their actions to be at all expressive of their real selves. But I do not think that these factors should change the penalty. I cannot remember one student who did not understand this point of view—or many parents, after it was explained to them. The important thing for them to know is that you make these distinctions in your own mind and tell them so.

Restoration and Confidence

Once the penalty is given, it is vital that the young person feel that she has not lost the confidence of the adult. As indicated before, young people want the adult world to believe in them, trust them, and love them—the generation gap notwithstanding.

"How can I ever trust her again?" a mother said to me, and I answered: "You have no choice. You have to keep on trusting her if you want her ever to become trustworthy. Once she decides you don't trust her any more, she will feel that there is no reason why she shouldn't act the way you expect her to act. You and I might find good reasons why she should behave well whether she is trusted or not, but they will not be her reasons. I cannot guarantee that she will act as she should because you trust her to do so, but I can guarantee that if you don't trust her she will certainly act as she shouldn't!"

But young people want more than your trust: they want your love also, regardless of what they do or say.

All of us have been baffled at times to discover that young people do not expect you to get angry with them and respond in kind when they criticize you and the institution you represent.

This is the other side of the Janus picture, the two-headed person looking forward to adulthood but when in trouble or lonely or upset scurrying back to the protection and forgiveness of childhood. When you are mowed down by the young and proceed to answer in kind, they look at you with wide, unbelieving, hurt eyes as if to say: "Sure, I was pretty nasty to you, but you have no right to be so unpleasant to me. I'm just a little girl (or boy), an itsy-bitsy kid. How could you be so unkind to me?"

I remember a new girl who griped incessantly about the school from the moment she arrived. Nothing was right about it. The work was too hard, the rules too petty, the teachers wouldn't help you—which, translated, means wouldn't do your work for you—and the girls kept her awake at night with their music and chatter. She would be glad when the year was over and she could hopefully persuade her parents to let her go back to her former school. If she had a good word to say for anything or anyone, including her roommate, I never heard it.

When the time came to send her parents a renewal blank for next year, I "forgot" to enclose hers in the mid-year report. A week later she stopped in to see me:

"Sir, my father said he didn't get a renewal blank for me. The other girls all got one."

"Well, Erica, I didn't send one."

"You didn't send one," she exclaimed, astonished and dismayed.

"Why, no, it never entered my head to send home a renewal blank. I have had the decided impression that you were very unhappy here. The assignments were too long, the work too hard, the teachers uninterested in helping you, the dormitories noisy. In fact, I believe you told someone that you couldn't wait to get out of this—quote —'dump'—unquote and get back to your former school where you could—quote 'raise hell' unquote and—quote 'have some fun'—unquote."

She looked very upset. "I don't think you want me back," she said sadly, as if the fact were incredible on the face of it!

"I want you back if you want to come back," I told her, "but I don't want your parents to drag you screaming into MacDuffie next September."

"This school isn't such a bad place," she said hopefully.

I smiled to myself.

"Look, little one," I said: "Why don't you think it over and come back to me exactly one week from now on Friday? I'll hold the place open."

"I might decide before that," she said.

"Well, think it over, and I'll see you next Friday."

She was in my office that afternoon.

"I've decided to come back," she said cheerfully.

"I'm very pleased," I said. "The renewal blank will be on its way tomorrow."

The next year I gave her a Little Sister (a new girl) to watch over and encourage during the first few weeks of school. I asked her the third week of school how her Little Sister was doing.

"Oh," she said, "she was pretty homesick at first, but I told her the school wasn't that bad, and I think she's coming around."

"I'm sure she is," I said solemnly.

Her parents had told me that she was very pleased that I had shown enough confidence in her loyalty to the school to give her a Little Sister. She wasn't about to gush to me, but I was perfectly content to have her saying to a new girl that the school wasn't "that bad." The young have to say it their way. Erica had done nothing "wrong" in griping, but taking her words at their face value had shaken her up and thrown her back on herself to make the decision she really wanted to make. In the broader meaning of the word, she had been "disciplined"—and restored.

What Kind of Trust?

We have talked a great deal about trust, but we must warn against the lazy "trust" that puts young people into situations of danger to them with a fatuous, "I trust you"; and the cowardly "trust" that is used to cover the reluctance of the parent or parent surrogate to investigate a disciplinary situation that might lead to a difficult and painful decision.

As a professional counselor, I have to remind parents that if they let their son drink at too early an age, on the happy grounds that they'd "rather have him drink at home," he just might decide that a martini with Mama wasn't really as much fun as two or three of them in a group of his own peers. Wouldn't you? And if your daughter can invite her boyfriend to your house and be alone with him for three or four hours at a time while you and your husband go out on your own, she just might get into trouble of some kind.

Trust is confidence in fundamental character, and the trust helps to produce the character itself. It is only old ladies of both sexes who believe that if they "trust" their children or their surrogate children without setting limits to protect their options, to prove their parental concern, and to stress their adult values, nothing can possibly happen to them, regardless of the circumstances.

Sure, you can't protect them completely. But many young people of high school age wish their parents would permit them to grow up more slowly until they are sure of their values rather than permit them to get into situations where they have to make decisions they are not yet prepared to make.

The fact that the students know that their word is believed unless you can *prove* that they are lying does *not* mean that you don't make a strong effort to get the truth. Many parents, principals, and headmasters don't really want to know the truth because they also know that unpleasant decisions will have to be made. If we feel it is important to teach young people to tell the truth, we *cannot encourage them to lie* by asking a casual question and then dismissing them in a rush lest they decide to come clean and cause us headaches. The parent or counselor who sets the stage for a quick and easy lie has no business congratulating himself for "trusting" the child or student. He is not trusting anyone; he is sacrificing the character of a young person on the altar of his own cowardice.

It is human to hope that suspicion of trouble will turn out to be false. But we have a commitment to the truth. We tell them we do not want a cat-and-mouse school, where we try to catch them and they attempt to evade us. However, we remind them that if we have reason to suspect them of something, we shall call them in, tell them what we know and what we don't know, and eventually ask them whether or not they have done this—whatever it may be.

You don't ask that final question right away. The student is told you will ask it, but first you remind him of the "trust" philosophy of the school; you tell him your hope, when you do ask him, that he will tell the truth because truth is the only thing that binds society, whether the school or the world, together; you say that if he admits he did this, you cannot let him out of the penalty, since you assume he is confessing because he wants to tell the truth and take his punishment; and you go over bit by bit whatever evidence you have.

What you are doing is two-fold: one, you are giving him time to make the decision that he alone will have to make since you don't have actual proof in most cases; second, you are letting him know without saying it or underscoring it that you are willing to accept the unpleasant responsibility of taking action if you have to; i.e., that *if you ask your students to be responsible, you will accept your own responsibilities as a parent, teacher, or counselor.*

Like the little freshman at college who was angry that her parents let her drift into a disturbing sexual relationship because they were fatuously trustful that she and her steady could be left alone together for years without falling into bed, young people expect us to be realistic and adult, while we trust them.

When we are asked, as we occasionally have been, how we can say we trust the students when we have a teacher sitting (not walking around) at the front of an examination room, we explain that we have never said that our trust was total. We want to protect the girls whose values are not yet wholly formed from being tempted to cheat, and we also want to equalize the examination so that the girl who does not cheat is supported in her honesty and not exploited by the girl who does.

Confession

In a school that stresses the ethical aspects of living together, some girl once in a while will want to confess to something of which you are totally unaware. Do you then become a priest or do you remain a headmaster?

The answer for me is that you are not a priest but a headmaster, that you cannot accept a blue-sky confession and do nothing about it.

So we say to our students, "We expect you to tell the truth, if asked about something; but we do not expect you to confess on your own because your conscience bothers you *unless you want to square yourself with the school society and your own regrets by accepting the usual penalty.*"

The word "usual" is the key one here. We don't want people to confess to something of which we have no knowledge in order to forestall a greater penalty if we happen to find it out, or none at all, as in some schools. Also, the girl who confesses only because her conscience bothers her is the kind of girl we want to keep in the school. We do not want her to confess to something that would compel us to suspend her or send her home. We also want to protect her from the emotional desire to feel psychologically cleansed by unburdening herself to a respected or loved father or mother figure in the community.

I might add that in lecturing on the psychology of discipline, I have had people in the audience who found it hard to believe that the young people of today would "confess" and risk punishment because of a desire to square themselves with the school and with themselves. This is part of the mythology of the sixties and seventies: that young people of today are a "different breed" from their predecessors. They are no different from their predecessors, but they operate in a different world—a world in which their elders are not certain of their own beliefs. They would be more sure of their values, if we were more sure of ours.

13 The Myths that Distort Reality

At the beginning of Chapter 9 I said, "Education is the quest for the real world." So far I have pictured this quest in terms of interpersonal relations: the kinds of expectations that we should have for young people in our communities of homes and school; the Third Ear method of understanding what they mean as opposed to what they say; assumptions about the generation gap; and a new emphasis on discipline and punishment as ways of teaching valuable lessons in the world of reality.

Interpersonal relations with their important emotional overtones are obviously not all there is to bringing up teenagers. Without slogging through the sand of educational theory, let me say that intellectually the job of school and home is to teach young people to *analyze problems, make distinctions, and come to conclusions.* In the school, the curriculum, whatever its content, is the material of this staggering process. In the home, all children, and especially teenagers, should be engaged in a continuous curriculum that has neither assignments nor marks. This curriculum is called conversation. The parents do not need to be professional teachers or have what is called "a good education." They need only to have the ability to think, convictions of their own, and sufficient confidence not to feel threatened when their children disagree with them. They also need to believe that teenagers are young adults and that their parents can neither talk down to them, shout at them, or tell them to grow up. Conversation with adults, practiced as a natural and interesting part of family living, is one of the ways in which young people do grow up. The conversations will not always be amicable. How could they be?

In both the school and the home the weapon of discussion is reason, buttressed as much as possible by knowledge and experience. The conversation should be horizontal, between equals, whether or not the knowledge, experience, and reason are equal.

We are of course aware that reason is an imperfect instrument; that equally sincere and intelligent people do not necessarily come to the same conclusions; that there are temperamental and environmental factors that predispose people to certain conclusions, which are then rationalized rather than reasoned out; that the world of experience in which ideas are tested is too varied and individual to be wholly reliable—but what of it? As teachers, what other method of coming to conclusions can we give?

We are adjured, and rightly so, not to teach mere facts without interpretation. We are passionately urged to teach our students to think. But once we have done so, we are exposed to a volley of objections to the thinking process. We are charged with indoctrination if the conclusion is contrary to what the critic believes, and a whole chorus of subjectivists remind us that the "visionary experience" is intuitive, magical, and not subject to scientific analysis.

I agree—but I don't consider this an argument against thinking. Nor do I believe that emotion—the great driving force in our lives—is less important than thought. Far from it. But it is different, and it is not enough, as our modern shamans would have us believe.

We tell our students that they should question all beliefs—including ours and theirs. We suggest that they be as critical of their college professors (especially if they are young and handsome!) as they have been of us; as critical of the Playboy philosophy as they have been of the church; as critical of their peers as they are of the older generation.

We also tell them to bring their theories to the test of experience as well as reason—including vicarious experience, since none of us can encompass the whole of life. We want to give them the tools of the critical intelligence, hoping that they will cut through the rah-rahs of the crowd and the persuasive verbiage of the articulate to the imprisoned reality that is waiting to be set free.

In a world that is crying for convictions from its leaders, we hope that they will not spend their lives juggling one belief against another in an endless game of "process" that stops short of any "production." Perpetually suspended belief is not a philosophy of life. Hopefully, they will eventually arrive at conclusions that will satisfy them intellectually, emotionally, and morally.

So we want to educate our young people to "reject the private myth," as Dr. Benson Snyder of MIT puts it, and subject themselves to a vigorous vis-à-vis with reality. In the process of analyzing the current mythology of our society, making distinctions, and coming to conclusions, they are going to find themselves battling, not only with the little quiet lies by which we live, but also with the clenched slogans of the articulate who demand in every medium that we hand over our minds to them. Accompanied, of course, by words and music.

The Myth of the Imposed Belief

The myth that to express a belief is to impose it is one of the distressing curiosities of the generation gap. It is not surprising that young people, clutching at their intellectual independence, should promulgate the myth, for which no rational basis can be found. The fact that large numbers of parents, misguided by pop intellectuals, have also accepted it has had a very disturbing effect on young people, whether or not they realize it. Increasing numbers of them do.

In the opening weeks of school I tell my students that I shall be expressing all year certain convictions I hold, and then add:

"Please don't tell me that I am imposing my beliefs on you. In a free school in a free society no one can impose a belief. If to impose is to establish or apply as compulsory or to make prevail by force, as the dictionary says, I could not possibly impose my beliefs on you. The only way I could do that would be to break down your nervous system by torture and absence of food, water, and sleep—as the totalitarian countries do.

"I can impose conduct on you, at least to the extent that I can make rules and set penalties; but I cannot impose my beliefs on you. Your minds are free to accept or reject whatever I say; and you can tell me I'm all wrong, and we can argue it out. But I'm going to say what I think, and I can impose on you the necessity of listening to me once a week. And I'll listen to you whenever you want me to; but I couldn't impose my beliefs on you if I tried, and please don't forget it."

This seems like a reasonably simple exercise in logic and adult-young people communication, but a great many parents seem to think it is taking a fearfully unfair advantage of an adolescent to express to him their own convictions; and a great many schoolmasters have followed suit. There is of course a genuine problem in the tax-supported public school, but where is the problem in the independent school? or in the home?

The problem is two-fold. Some parents are not sure enough of their own beliefs to be willing to express them with passionate conviction, but these parents are in the minority. Almost all the parents that I have worked with had strong beliefs about right and wrong, but they hesitated to express them because of the fear they were encroaching on their children's freedom to choose their own beliefs.

This must be the first society in history where a large number of parents decided that they have no right to explain their own beliefs and practices to the younger generation. It is ironic that at a time when communication is at an all-time high, when the flood tide of information and ideas from television, movies, radio, newspapers, books, plays, articles, and speeches pours into our houses and slowly rises into every inlet of our minds, parents who could be communicating to their children what they have learned from the knowledge explosion and especially from the experience of living are cultivating their gardens, whether of social life, community service, or church work, and letting other people tell their teenagers what they should believe in.

That this is done from the noblest cliché of all, "I want my child to make up his own mind about right and wrong," does not alter the fact that it is parental abdication, and, further, that it leaves the young people, who have supposedly been blessed by such loving and liberal renunciations, angry, confused, and contemptuous.

Looking out of my office window, all I could see were six or seven girls, surrounding a stranger. The stranger had a big shock of uncombed hair and an old sweater on. Wondering if trouble of some sort were brewing, I stepped out of the office and started toward the group. The stranger had dirty blue jeans, cut open at each knee, with bits of colored cloth sewed on at various places. Her sneakers had large holes in the canvas.

One of the girls saw me coming. "It's Gale," she said excitedly, "back from college."

It was indeed Gale, and I hoped she didn't notice my look of surprise.

"Hello, little one," I said, "come into the office and tell me about college."

We sat down, and she grinned.

"I don't look like your last year's president of Student Council, do I?"

"You're wearing the college uniform of this year. I don't care about your clothes. Tell me about yourself."

"I'm turning my books in at Christmas," she said. "I'm quitting college."

"Why?"

"I'm tired of pounding books. I did it for four years at MacDuffie, and I don't want four more years of it." She was on the defensive and her voice was sharper than at first.

"How do your parents feel about it?"

"They want me to do whatever I think best. It's up to me."

"That makes it tougher, doesn't it?" I said.

She shrugged her shoulders.

"I never know what they think anyway. It's always up to me."

"You know they don't want you to quit college, and neither do I."

"Why don't they say so, then?" she snapped. "Why don't they tell me what they really think?" She ignored the "neither do I."

"They don't want to interfere with you," I said, "but no parent wants a bright girl like you to give up college. What are you going to do?"

"I don't know yet. I want to get a job. I want to do something. I'm sick of libraries. I'm sick of being a cooperative citizen, or president of Student Council. I want to be uncooperative and a bad influence."

I laughed.

"Well, you're not Student Council President in college," I said. "Let's look at your options. What kind of job do you think you're going to get only one year out of high school? And where do you want to live?"

"New York City," she said firmly. "I'll live in the Village."

"What kind of job do you think you can get in New York? Let's be realistic."

We argued it back and forth for quite a while. Sometimes I felt she was about to agree, but at other times I didn't think I was getting anywhere.

A month later she told me she had quit college and was looking for a job. I didn't hear from her for a year-and-a-half, and then I got a letter:

Dear RDR,

I think it's about time I wrote you a letter. In the first place, I want you to know that I am not your ideal MacDuffie girl, and you wouldn't be inclined to list me as the Student Council President who best represents the ideals of the school.

In the year that I've been working—at a lousy job—I've been through the sex bit and I've been through the drug bit, and you might as well know it.

Sir, I want to get back into some college, and you're the only person who can help me. May I use you as a reference?

We had a good talk when I saw you. I knew what you would say when I went up there, and I guess I rather hoped you would persuade me, but when I got back it still seemed pretty thrilling to be on my own. It didn't turn out to be that thrilling.

> I wish my parents had told me not to leave college. I wish they had gotten angry and told me I was a fool. I have wasted almost two years of my life. Why are parents so afraid to tell their kids what they think?

Why, indeed?

The Myth That Articulate People Are Wise

Anyone who teaches English, as I have, discovers how persuasive the written word is in the hands of a literary artist. When so many adults form their opinions, not by the content of speeches and articles, but by the impact of the speaker and the style of the writer, it is no wonder that young people make the same mistake. Parents can be especially valuable in analyzing the contents of our current mythology and pointing out its logical deficiencies to their children.

The school also has an important part to play in showing students how to analyze statements, make distinctions, and come to conclusions. Although the public school is more limited than the private one in stating its own conclusions, both institutions are certainly free to teach logical analysis to their students. In fact, I know of no school, public or private, which does not consider its curriculum a means of teaching young people to think for themselves —which, by inference, means to stop letting the myth-makers and the cliché mongers think for them.

Articulate people may or may not be wise. No matter how bright the packaging—perhaps because it is so bright; no matter how charismatic the personality—perhaps because it is so attractive; a writer, speaker, publicist, or pundit must be continually submitted to the scrutiny of the analytical mind, or we'll be ready for Big Brother in and after 1984.

Heather was an excellent English student, with a range and depth of reading unusual in an eleventh grader.

She was the daughter of a teacher and books had been part of her growing up. She had just discovered the perverse genius of Jean Genet and the "candid vision of evil" he imposed.

"Have you read him?" she asked with excitement. How well I remembered the same excitement on my part when I encountered as a high school student the radical writers of my youth.

"I've read *The Thief's Journal*," I told her, "and Sartre's essay on "Saint Jean." There's no doubt it's fascinating to explore a mind like Genet's. He writes beautifully."

"He has such a wonderful philosophy!" she exclaimed.

"Well, Heather, you can admire a writer's style and be fascinated by his exaltation of everything we consider wrong, and you can be angry at the kind of brutal and deprived life that made him a thief, but I hardly see how you can find his philosophy 'wonderful.' "

"Don't you think he makes evil saintly? He shows the hypocrisy of our own morality by discovering beauty in being a criminal. He says he wants to construct a new moral order."

"I know he says it. But what kind of moral order is he really constructing? You remember he glorifies betrayal, theft, and homosexuality."

"Yes, I think I do."

"I'm not trying to preach you a sermon. It expands our knowledge and compassion to read this man's story, the life of a male prostitute to sailors, when we know that he was an illegitimate child and an orphan, sent to a reformatory when he was ten. The style and the power and the content make a remarkable book, but hardly produce a 'wonderful philosophy.' "

We discussed some incidents in the book, which is autobiographical.

"Do you remember when he tied the hands of the man

who had invited him to a homosexual act, and after robbing him, smashed him in the face and reveled in the 'amazing power' the blow had given, 'not only to my body, but to my mind'? I don't think you would accept as wonderful the philosophy that would glory in smashing a helpless man's face in order to give one a sense of power."

I did not ask her to admit verbally that the new moral order of Genet was one without pity and without guilt, even for murder. As I said earlier, you hand back a young person's pride when you state your point and assume she can understand it without beating her to her knees with your adult logic and knowledge. You are trying to teach her to love critical analysis, not to brush it aside because she has been humiliated by yours. Once she looks beyond her own mind and moral sense to the beauty of the words woven around the ugliest of actions, she is ready to join the great cloud of romantics who view the bitterest of reality through word-covered glasses.

Parents do not need to be literary critics to look beyond the words to the reality. And to teach their children to do the same. Literature is the expression of experience, and as such can enlarge our own. But inarticulate people have had experience, too, and they know that the person who is robbed and smashed has found no beauty in the process; the person who is betrayed does not discover moral beauty in treachery; and the persons who buy and sell bodies, whether for hetero- or homosexual desires, are planting no roses in the garden of sex. Compassion, yes; but admiration, hardly.

Bonnie and Clyde played in Springfield quite a while after the letter in *Time* from the college freshman who came crying out of some theater and exclaimed: "They belong to our generation. We identify with all outlaws."

Would she have identified with them if her father had

been the bank teller whom Clyde shot down and killed for the bank's money?

As I went out of the theater, I could see that the audience was moved by the riddled body of Bonnie, Faye Dunaway of the long hair and the lovely face. A broad-beamed woman, with a kind and empty face, who looked like the apple pie mom of the All-American home, was saying to her friend, "He just wouldn't leave them alone; he just kept going after them" She was referring, with great indignation, to the law officer who finally tracked down her beloved screen criminals. Movies are great mythmakers, and they need to be analyzed by the realistic mind.

I gave a chapel talk the next day on *Bonnie and Clyde*, using some of the material from John Toland's excellent article on "The Real Bonnie and Clyde" in the *New York Times Magazine.* I contrasted the two as they really were with the romantic Warren Beatty and Faye Dunaway and suggested that the students might identify with the victim of the two murderers and their families.

We discussed it at dinner that night. This kind of discussion should go on constantly in the home. Outwardly, the teenagers may not agree with you, but you have nonetheless made your point. Don't let the movies, the magazines, and television make all the points for you. Or the posters.

I was walking through the corridor of one of the dorms the next day and saw a huge poster of Bonnie and Clyde on the wall opposite the open door of one of the rooms. Underneath the student had written, "We love Bonnie and Clyde."

She had bought it after my chapel talk the day before. Such role playing is nothing to get angry about. I had made my point and that was all I could do.

One of the hardest things for parents to do is to let a matter drop. Admittedly, when it is your child and you are indignant, you want to be *sure* you have gotten the point over, and so you repeat it and hammer it in and pound it home until the argument you might have won has only built up a wall of resistance that is founded, not on logic, but on irritation, weariness, and reaction. With teenagers especially, it is wise to state your point, with all the reason and emotion and impact you can give it—and then change the subject. Assume that, at least on reflection, your teenager is going to agree. She can't reflect while you are running backwards over the same ground.

The Myth That Feeling Is Enough

We live at a time when feeling is apotheosized as the touchstone of reality. "What is moral is what you feel good after, and what is immoral is what you feel bad after," is the stark ethics of our greatest novelist, Hemingway. And Henry Miller is proud to announce, "All my life I have felt a great kinship with the madman and the criminal." With the massive simplicity of the subjective, he assures us that "civilization is rotten" and begs us to "release the instinctive vitality of the primitive." I want to be there when someone releases the instinctive vitality of the primitive on Henry Miller and beats him up for his money or his watch.

"A riot makes one feel alive, primitive, and vitally whole again," but that's not how the victim of the riot feels:

the gutted store . . .

the broken back . . .

the book of a lifetime's work burned . . .

the quiet body in the street . . .

"The boys kill the frogs in sport, but the frogs do not die in sport." Feeling is not enough.

I am talking to Julie, whose roommate had taken French leave of the school.

"I have a note from Betty that she's headed for home. Did you know about it?"

"Yes, sir. She has been talking about it for a long time."

"When did she leave?"

"Early this morning."

"I'm really disappointed. She had made such great strides in her work, and she seemed to be accepting the fact that Dave was quite a distance away and couldn't visit the school often. I think she should have stayed and graduated."

"But, sir, she couldn't stay."

"Couldn't? Why not?"

"Because she just felt she *had* to go. That was the way she *felt*."

"Are you telling me she is going to marry Dave?"

"Oh, no, Dave isn't such a big deal in the situation. She was just fed up with the school and everything. She just felt she *had* to leave."

"Her father has already paid half the bill for her tuition here: $1,750. That amount of money for a month in the school is pretty expensive, and he's really responsible for the whole bill legally, although I wouldn't ask him for it. Don't you think she owed him something?"

"But, sir, you can't force a person to stay somewhere against her will."

"I didn't say you could. I just asked you whether you didn't think she had some obligation toward her parents."

"But she also had an obligation to herself."

"That wasn't my question."

"I don't think we're going to agree on this. You're talking to me as if I had run away. I'm still here."

I smiled.

"Yes, I know. Do you mind if I ask you a couple of other questions?"

"Go ahead."

"You're applying for Early Decision to college. I have to have your recommendation in by November 1."

She looked puzzled—and concerned.

"Aren't you going to recommend me?"

"Of course I am."

"Then what is the question?"

"Did you ever consider the possibility that I might like to run away?"

She laughed. "You, sir?"—as if it were the ultimate incredibility. "From this school?"

"Sure, why not? I get fed up."

She looked very surprised. "You do?"

"Of course I do. It isn't the easiest thing in the world to be a headmaster, with both boarders and day pupils. Writing reports to the colleges is one of my hardest jobs. I must be honest and give weaknesses as well as strengths. Your generation admires honest people—yes? Even if my honesty kept you out of the college of your choice—yes? That's a pretty feeble nod of the head, but at least it's in the right direction. Thanks. Anyway, if all seventy of you apply on an average to 3.7 colleges, I shall have written almost 260 detailed reports on you, and meanwhile the school goes on with problems to be solved, decisions to be made, people to be seen. Why shouldn't I write one brief harmless paragraph on each of you, and just have it typed for every college, regardless of difference in academic standards? And why shouldn't I just split after a few seventy-hour weeks. Go to Nassau. Head for Europe. To hell with all you kids."

"But, sir, if you don't mind my saying so, you are paid to do those things."

"I'm not really paid to work as hard as I do, or to be as perfectionistic about your college reports as I am. But what's that got to do with it? You were arguing that Betty had to leave because that's the way she felt. So maybe that's the way I feel. So why shouldn't I leave?"

You never push an argument like this beyond a certain point. You don't keep demanding answers until the young person is battered into a corner. You're not trying to show your students your intellectual muscle. It is important to let them make the final conclusions to your arguments. They're bright or they wouldn't be in your school. Your job is to get them to think carefully, realistically, about any proposition. You have to sense when it's time for you to withdraw your arguments, and let their minds take over. "Don't you agree with me?" is a phrase I rarely use. Let them agree inside and preserve their sense of privacy and independence.

I didn't pursue the matter further with the roommate. I called Betty and told her I thought she ought to return. It was a long phone call, but she finally decided that she would. I thanked her and hung up.

I met her as she got out of the taxi.

"Welcome home," I said. "It's nice to have you back."

"Shall I tell the taxi to wait?" she asked.

"Why should it wait? Didn't you pay the driver?"

She looked at me curiously—as if she were trying to figure me out for the first time.

"I paid him all right," she said, "but I thought you might like to have him drive *you* to the station. Julie says you get the urge to split, too."

I laughed, and so did she.

Every year a fine local college holds a Model Congress for high school students throughout Western Massachusetts. Each high school may bring one bill to be voted on by the Congress. This particular year, one school presented a bill to sterilize all mothers after they had had two children, in order to check the population explosion and help create a world where all people would have enough food to eat. One can hardly quarrel with a desire to eliminate starvation from the world. But emotion, even with the finest of goals, is not enough. There are other questions. We discussed them at the school.

Laura was the proponent, a fiery, very intelligent proclaimer of women's rights.

Laura: To have more than two children is immoral and should not be permitted.

The question-answer period below has been edited to give the most significant exchanges between Laura and the other students.

Student: Why should you decide what is immoral for other people? If you only want two children, have two. Maybe I want three.

Laura: Scientists say that having only two children would mean that the world's resources could take care of all children—not just the children of the rich. Overpopulation also affects the environment adversely.

Student: You say "scientists" as if all scientists agreed with your point of view. People are always saying, "Scientists, educators, sociologists agree." I don't believe it. What scientists are you talking about?

Laura mentioned an article she had read, which I have forgotten.

Student: You believe then that every mother should be sterilized after she has had two children.

Laura: Yes, I do. For the good of the whole community.

Student: But that's what Hitler said when he killed the Jews.

Laura: The fact that evil men have used the good of the community or the state as an excuse to kill or torture other people does not mean that the idea isn't a good one. Every good idea has been abused by someone.

Student: Don't you think this is giving the government great power? It is really giving them the power of life and death.

Laura: Nobody's being killed. People just aren't being born.

Student: Suppose the government decides that mothers should have only one child, or none at all. Once you give the government the power to decide how many children can be born, you can't guarantee that it will be limited to two. What about the rights of the mother? Don't married men and women have the right to create life?

Laura: Would you give that right to two people who were criminally insane if scientists knew that the offspring would be insane also?

Student: I'm not sure scientists know such things. I would not deprive anyone of the right to create life.

Laura: How about a man in the advanced stages of syphilis, who would certainly give birth to a blind child? Why should people be allowed to give birth to a child who will starve because there are too many children in the world?

Student: This wouldn't happen in America, and you couldn't prove that they would starve anyway.

Laura: What about Africa? Maybe African babies wouldn't starve if there were fewer people in other parts of the world.

Thinking is hard work. People were getting tense. It wasn't just a debate any more. We were talking about ourselves.

Student: Suppose a mother has two children and she's sterilized. And the two children are killed in an auto accident. You have not given her the right to have two children. You have decreed that she can have none.

Laura hesitated for the first time.

Laura: That would be a very unfortunate accident —not too likely to occur. It has to be the greatest good for the greatest number.

Student: Suppose a mother has two children; her

husband dies or is divorced. She marries another man. The state is depriving them by this law of the most fundamental of human rights—the right to express their love by having children of their own, by having a family. The state is just a bunch of politicians. What right have they got to tell a husband and wife what kind of a home, or no home, they can have? If they are given this right, they'll ask for more rights over the personal lives of people. What kind of a country would this be with all this government power? Pretty soon they'd be telling us whether we could get married or not. It's ridiculous!

Student: Suppose a woman refuses to be sterilized.

Laura: Of course she has to obey the law.

Student: Suppose she goes to prison for her rights. Would you keep her there for life?

Laura: Of course not.

Student: How long would you keep her there?

Laura: I'd try to persuade her to change her point of view.

Student: But that's brainwashing.

Laura: Brainwashing is just a word. Aren't we brainwashed here?

Several girls looked at me. "We can argue that some other time," I said, "Let's get back to the subject."

Student: So your brainwashing doesn't work. You'll have to sterilize her by force, won't you?

Laura: I guess so.

Student: Would you hold her down while it was being done? Would you do it by force? Yourself?

The Model Congress voted down the proposal that after two children, a woman should be sterilized by the state. The margin wasn't as big as some of us would have liked. At least at MacDuffie, we brought out some pretty hard implications of the emotional desire to do good. We also touched base on one of the great moral myths, namely, that the end justifies the means. We hadn't had at that time the clean-cut, earnest young faces of Watergate.

The cult of feeling has some rather frightening byways in today's youth culture. Too great a respect for how another person "feels" about something may lead to an almost total lack of responsibility for that other person's action. That kind of responsibility is considered an invasion of privacy; a manipulation; an inexcusable unwillingness to let an individual do his thing. The paradox is that today's young people are far more concerned about their fellow men and women than previous groups. Young people and their older counterparts who do not want to "interfere" with anyone's lifestyle or freedom of action will tenderly pick you up and care for you unstintingly after you have jumped out the window, but they won't necessarily try to stop you from jumping!

I had had to expel Peggy. A pretty, thoughtless youngster of sixteen, she had made a habit of climbing down the fire escape late at night to meet a group of college boys in a rooming house near the college. She assured me that nothing had "happened," and I was glad to believe it; that there were college girls there; that all they did was drink beer, smoke, and sit around. However, the school rule was explicit and the reasons for it had been given many times.

Expulsion is traumatic, no matter how you may try to soften it. And you do try.

But it is still a very sad occasion, especially when the girl who thought she didn't care about the school suddenly discovers, when the mask is down, that she really loves it; when the family, who has pictured their daughter walking down the long white line of graduation, knows that this is no longer possible but still tells you that they understand your position and will always praise the school;

when the girls are crying and Peggy comes in to say goodbye to you and thanks you for all you've done for her . . .
and she writes you a wonderful letter afterward, and you
hope she knows how much you care about her and how
hard it was to do what you had to do. And suddenly you're
very angry at all the girls in the school who are now weeping because Peggy has to leave, and you say to yourself:
"Why in hell didn't someone at least warn her? Everyone
but the prefects must have known that she was going out
two and three times a week for many weeks."

So you call in a few of your most sensitive, mature,
and thoughtful girls. One conversation will be about the
same as all the others.

"Hi, Bea."

"Hi, sir."

"I feel very sad about Peggy's going."

"We all do, sir. She was really a good kid."

"I know she was. I was surprised to find out how long
this had been going on. Didn't you girls know about it?"

"Most of the older girls knew. I don't know about the
younger ones."

"Of course I tell you at the beginning of the year that
no girl ever has to report another girl. I wouldn't ask girls
of your age to turn each other in. That is too painful to the
girl who does it, and I know it would alienate her from the
whole peer group. On the other hand, I hope that somebody warned Peggy of the danger of what she was doing
even if you didn't want to call it wrong; that someone told
her that she was bound to get caught in time—and why
not stop while she was ahead? If I were a fellow-student,
I'd be glad that I talked like that to her. If she didn't follow my advice, I at least had done my part. I had warned
her. I had told her to cut it out."

"But, sir, this was *her* decision, not anyone else's. No
one forced her to break the rules. She knew what the

penalty was. It was her decision. That was the way she *felt*."

There it was again.

"Don't you think people ever change their mind? Don't you realize that sometimes they need support from their friends to break away from a foolish act or habit that can lead to harm of some sort, even tragedy, for them? These were college boys; Peggy probably was flattered to be going with them. There was a certain excitement in breaking an important rule. The very danger of getting caught added to the excitement. She needed someone to wake her up. Someone who cared for her. Like her friends. Someone to say: 'Look, Peggy, cut it out. What are you thinking of? Someone is likely to spill it, even by mistake. You're going to get caught sometime and be expelled. Is it really worth that to you?' What is so dreadful about saying that? Wouldn't you feel better if you had?"

Bea was upset and close to tears. I knew I was giving her a hard time—after the fact. I knew she would have been one of the most likely girls to have warned Peggy. That was why I had picked her out for this talk. I had hoped that she might have said something to Peggy. But obviously she hadn't.

"It's not as easy, sir, as you seem to think. It's not easy at all." Her voice broke and she tried to control it. "It's easy for you," she said, as if she were accusing me of something. "It's easy for you!" Her voice rose sharply. "Don't you understand? *They're one of us, they're one of us! How can we tell them what to do?*"

She sobbed as if she would never stop.

My mind went back to the high school in California where more than half the school knew that one of their number, a dropout, had murdered two girls. They didn't turn him in. Eventually, he murdered a third, and the authorities caught him.

The two most important experiences of young people in the last fifteen years were Vietnam and Woodstock. The unity of opposition and the unity of comradeship. The war is over and the spirit of Woodstock died in Altamont when the blades flashed in the hands of Hell's Angels and even the music of Mick Jagger could not hide the fact that two young men had been beaten to death.

"Please don't cry," I said to Bea, "please don't cry. I understand."

The Myth of the Superhuman Young Person

Our speakers and writers have deafened our ears for well over a decade with the far from uncertain sound of the trumpet extolling the virtues of youth. The Chaplain of a famous women's college assures us that youth is forging a new kind of morality and that no one over twenty-five can possibly understand it. (Since he himself is over twenty-five, he ought to turn in his collar and try to find work that he *does* understand.)

The Myth of the Superhuman Young Person has flowered in the home, the school, and society. Parents have had good reasons to be timid and apologetic. Youth was "The Man of the Year" on the cover of *Time Magazine* for January 6, 1967. It was pretty hard to ask the Man of the Year to pick up a loaf of bread at the store.

Several years ago a nearby high school dedicated the senior yearbook to themselves in the following words: "We have the potential of no other generation that has gone before. . . . We shall continue to question, because here lies our greatness. . . . And it is to us, to the potential that is ours, and to the tomorrow that is ours, that we dedicate this yearbook." What could a loving parent do but fade away as quickly as possible so the young could take over?

High school young people did not read the serious historians and interpreters of the youth movement: Erikson, Keniston, Hook, Roszak, Friedenberg, Goodman,

Aldridge and others, any more than their collegiate counterparts wrestled over the labored grammar of Marcuse—but
they got the message. They were a new breed, with a new
kind of consciousness, according to the author of *The
Greening of America*; they had the courage, vision, commitment and what-have-you to change the world—in a
year or two. The proper posture of the older generation was
to earnestly repent and to be heartily sorry, in the quaint
words of the prayerbook, for these their misdoings—in
presenting their children with an imperfect world.

Although they publicly accepted the homage of the
youth worshippers of the postwar period, inwardly young
people were very disturbed by it and by their own inability to live up to their billing as "the most *this* and the
most *that* that ever was in the world," to quote Panta-
gruel in Rabelais, exalting his dead wife Badebec when
more specfic words of praise eluded him.

But Badebec was dead. Our teenagers were alive and
facing every day the challenge to be as superhuman in
their achievements as their admirers insisted they should
be, and were. It was tough going.

They began to develop a fear of being human. They
must excel in everything they did. They were wired to win.

She came into my office after school, sat down, and
started to cry. Since I had seen her looking perfectly calm
at lunch, I did not think that any tragedy had enveloped
her family, but of course one never knows. Perhaps the
news had come by telephone, although I had always in the
past been called before the girl was if there was serious
trouble at home.

I let her cry.

"What's the matter?" I finally asked her.

"I don't know," she said in desperation.

"You don't know why you're upset?"

She looked as if she might start all over again.

"I really don't, sir. I just feel awful. Please believe me."

"Of course I believe you. Maybe you could think of some word besides 'awful.' Like lonely, or unappreciated, or scared?"

"None of them," she said. "I just feel awful."

I tried again. "Awful what?"

"Awful—," she hesitated. "I don't know. Awful useless, I guess."

"Why 'useless'?"

"I'm useless," she said, her voice rising, "useless. I can't do anything. I can't do anything at all."

"You're a fine artist," I said. "I have no talent in that at all. You wrote a one-act play last year that was one of five put on in assembly. I thought it was excellent (and I did). It was imaginative, sensitive, well-written."

"I had forgotten that," she said, "but I'm not any great student."

"You're an honor student in a college preparatory school. You're not an A student, but what of it? We want your best, that's all. It just happens that your best is good. What's bothering you? We're very pleased with you and your work. Was there anything that triggered all this? Did you get a low grade in some test?"

"No," she said, "but I don't seem to be as bright as some girls."

I suddenly remembered that the day before I had announced in assembly the girls who were semifinalists in the National Merit contest.

"Pat," I said, "did you begin to feel upset when I announced the girls who were semifinalists in the National Merit contest?"

"I don't think so," she said hesitantly, "but maybe that reminded me."

We both smiled.

The fear of being human . . . of having defects. It is an

insidious fear, as fear usually is, and a dangerous one. The ability to accept one's limitations and at the same time rejoice in what one *can* do is a sign of healthy human nature.

How many children have been told sententiously, "You can do anything if you really want to and are willing to try hard enough." That is a crippling myth, a disheartening lie. The parent who says this knows it isn't true, but he hopes that the challenge to achieve an impossible goal may bring his child at least nearer that goal. He is pitifully and permanently wrong, unless his goals for his children are discouragement, a low self-concept, or an image based on fantasy instead of fact.

We call the latter, in the words of Karen Horney, "the idealized image." A young person who has been subjected to the more starry-eyed writers and speakers on "youth" is likely to develop an idealized image of herself as perpetually victorious over life's problems. She gets all As. She is beautiful, charming, sweet (in her dreams). She knocks men dead at 100 yards. They sweep her into their arms (later on, when reality sets in, she's doing most of the sweeping).

I think of all the compulsive, unhappy success hunters I have worked with—nice kids who had been convinced by some parent or pundit that they were superhuman and not only must not fail at anything but must be spectacularly successful in whatever they did. I am *not* talking about normal disappointment over failing to make some office or honor. I am talking about the person who consistently overrates his or her potential and equates worth with success or failure in reaching that potential.

I remember the girls who worked so hard to get into what they considered a prestige college that they found out they hated it once they arrived. I am convinced that one of the reasons for the rise of the drug traffic in the years of student rebellion was the desire to "feel" successful and superhuman after being finally confronted with the un-smashable face of reality.

To the human being who feels laid upon him the compulsion to be first, the idealized image of himself must be preserved at all costs. From this group come the overcompensating Hitlers, and all the great and inglorious group of tense, unhappy, rigid people who build up defenses against their failures to be superhuman, walls of rationalization, overcompensation, and fantasizing—with exits of escape into mythology, mental breakdown, alcohol, and drugs.

I remember walking through a dormitory at one of those tense times before the seniors have heard from their college choices. On the wall of one of the rooms was a placard with the words:

"They said it couldn't be done. But he rolled up his sleeves, spat on his hands, tackled the thing that couldn't be done—and he couldn't do it!"

I blessed that girl....

At my high school graduation, the speaker told us, "You are the Hope of the World." It is the only graduation address I remember, except a few that I have given. It was pretty exciting to be the hope of the world. Have you looked at the world lately?

I used this title in one of my assembly talks. I pictured a young person who had just heard the speech—in my generation of course—expostulating with his mother:

"Look, Ma, I'm the hope of the world. Don't ask me to mow the lawn—I'm the hope of the world. Don't ask me to wash the dishes—I'm the hope of the world."

I ended the talk by suggesting to the students: "Why don't you let the world go for a couple of weeks? Try for one week to be the hope of your roommate. Try next fall to be the hope of that homesick new girl, who sees all the oldtimers like you laughing and joking, and feels left out and shy and afraid. Be the hope of your parents. Tell them every once in a while what's happy about your school experience and don't save all the gripes for your phone calls and letters to them. They have a right to enjoy themselves, just like you and me. You might even try being the hope of your headmaster. I feel pretty hopeless myself once in a while and I say to myself, 'What's a nice boy like me doing in a place like this!' "

There were smiles of amusement, and, I am very sure, of relief also. When Desdemona, shocked by Othello's accusation of infidelity, asks the more sophisticated Emilia whether she would commit adultery for the whole world, Emilia replies, "The world's a huge place."

It is, indeed, and the young generation find it hard to be the most wonderful human beings that have ever graced it—as their panegyrists expect them to be.

The idealized image must give way to the reality of one's limitations, to one's real self. The latter will inevitably be less glamorous than the idealized image, but it will be easier to live with in the long run. At the same time that we are gently, firmly bringing the student face to face with what Emerson calls "the rough, electric shocks of truth," we are softening the impact of those shocks by holding the mirror up to the real qualities of mind and heart and talent that will make her a strong and happy person. She does not see the many hands that hold the mirror. She does not even know the mirror is there. But the subtle, enveloping process has begun with administration, faculty, parents, and house parents to support her in disappointment, while we build her up in approval; to dispel the myths that distort reality while we help create the real person—at her best.

The Myth of Relativism

The Myth of Relativism is the result of the morbid fear of absolutes that characterizes the modern mind. People who have decided ideas about politics, commerce, economics, and education develop rubbery moral legs at the very thought of taking a firm stand on any of the problems of right and wrong that beset—one might almost say besiege —our society.

An actor in *The Godfather* praises in the *New York Times* the sense of family shown by the Corleones in spite of a vivid picture of adultery with a simpering partner backed up against a wall, while later on one of the family's in-laws is garroted with a wire as he sits in the front seat of a car.

To the relativist there is no such thing as right or wrong. To quote a popular song of my generation, "it all depends on you," or on the custom of the country or group, "the street where you live." Since the word moral comes from the Latin *mos, moris*, which means "custom," right and wrong are purely matters of custom. Just like that.

We are having a discussion of right and wrong, and one of the girls says to me:

"Well, sir, I may not think that something is right, but if someone thinks it's right, it's right for her."

The second comment is like the first:

"Sir, you think your ideas are right, but other people equally sincere think their ideas are right"—the implication being that ideas are equally valid if sincerely held.

The trouble is that these sentiments, generous as they sound, just don't hold up in real life, i.e., reality. I remind my students that if a mugger approaches them with a knife and intent to rob, beat, and possibly murder them, they are not going to tell him sweetly, "I don't think what you're doing is right, but if you think it's right, it's right for you." At that moment, the most sincere relativist becomes an absolutist, and if she has any voice at all it will be used to tell her assailant that it is wrong for him to attack her and that his sincerity is not adequate excuse for the crime he is about to commit.

Or I may remind the student that if she were so unfortunate as to meet a headhunter, if any of them now exist, who with passionate religious conviction believed that he was doing "the will of God" by relieving her of her head, she would not be about to tell him that she had great respect for his beliefs because he was so "sincere" about them.

It was Sinclair Lewis who commented with typical fervor: "Sincere? Hell! So is a cockroach." Who can say that Hitler was not sincere? Six million dead bear quiet witness to his love of the undefiled Aryan state.

Myths About Sex

To discuss sex as part of a chapter in a book about teenagers would appear to be giving one of the most important subjects in the world a wholly insufficient amount of space. However, to analyze sex and the teenager at length is to write a second book before finishing the first.

I once told an expectant audience that I had written a two-line, three-word poem that encapsulated the entire history of sex. The poem:

Sex
Is Complex

The "How To" in the title of this book indicates suggestions, but it does not promise *your* answer. The only answer I can give is *my* answer, and I give it. The only universal advice I can give parents and counselors is, "Say it." Tell them what you really believe at all costs. As my friend and fellow headmaster Ned Hall said once, "It is wrong to conceal one's moral position, and dishonest to falsify it." Young people want to know where we stand, although they may make every effort to batter down our platform and send us reeling to the ground.

In dealing with teenagers, it is not enough to answer a question with a question. In an article in *Look Magazine*,

Dr. Mary Calderone was asked by a boy what she believed about premarital sex. "What do you believe about it?" she shot back, and this was supposed to be a significant answer. In the same article, Wallace Fulton, President of SIECUS, tells how he would handle a young boy and girl who wanted to know what was wrong with having intercourse. Mr. Fulton would ask them the following questions: "How old are you? Why do you want to have intercourse?" (Oh, come on, Mr. Fulton!) "Why can't you get married?" He then goes on to explain, "Only in marriage will society be in total support."

You remember—or at least I do—the famous cartoon in *The New Yorker*, I believe. The couple involved had obviously been having a romantic session on the couch. As the boy comes up for air, his hair tousled, a wild, faraway look in his eye, he blurts out to the girl, "Have you read any good books lately?"

The cartoon in a slightly different sense could be applied to Mr. Fulton's grave pronouncement. It is hard to picture a boy or a girl, after the heady preliminaries of sex, asking one another just before its consummation, "Do you realize that society will not be in total support?"

So what do we tell our kids about sex? Is there any common denominator for those with opposing theories? I think there is for all but an unreconcilable few. I'll talk about fundamental principles rather than the myriad of specific questions I've been asked in both boys' and girls' schools.

Whatever one's personal convictions may be, the specifically religious approach to sex is not accepted today by the great majority of students. The headmaster of a school, unlike a parent in this respect, faces young people of all varieties of religious and moral beliefs. So in sex, as in every other subject, we start with where the teenagers are, not where we might like them to be.

Of all perceptive people, teenagers as a group are the most perceptive. That is not because they are young but because their beliefs have not been fully established, and they are trying to evaluate the adult society and its answers to their questions. We adults may have kept our I.Q., our intelligence quotient; but most of us have not retained the Q.Q. of youth, the quest quotient. It is the Q.Q. that keeps people perceptive.

Even if we feel that our privacy is invaded by their questions, it's a friendly invasion, affectionate, sometimes surprised (sex is supposed to belong to them, not us!), always appreciative of our frankness. They want to know what we really believe, not what we think we are supposed to say—and what we live, not what we profess.

By the way, they will often protect their own privacy, with the greatest of care. They will invite you in if they want to, but an invitation is not promised. Nor should it be sought. The questions they ask will be asked from a seemingly lofty, intellectual, objective height—as if knowledge were their only consideration. But what they really are asking about is meaning.

It is hard to find meaning until we have dispelled myth.

The Myth That Sex Is Overemphasized in Our Culture

The so-called sexual revolution of modern times is widely supposed by its opponents to have created a tragic overemphasis on sex. The proponents of the revolution claim that they are only reacting against the crushing puritanism of earlier views.

Mythology begins to take over.

Some of us, traveling widely in every section of the country for the last twenty years, have looked in vain for this crushing Puritanism. It has been hard to find, but it must be there, if only we can discover where "there" is located. The dragon is still at large, we are constantly told, and the St. Georges of the new morality are ever on the alert, to protect us from it.

Except for those kind hearts and gentle people who still believe that the sexual revolution is more verbal than actual, there is general agreement that there has been a great increase in sexual activity among young people in the last fifteen or twenty years. As a counselor of young people, both in school and out, I could hardly deny it.

On the other hand, I affirm that instead of an over-emphasis on sex in our society we are witnessing a tragic deemphasis. Before I am certified as a fugitive from a mental hospital, let me differentiate between sex and the act of sex; and here is where the battle is really joined.

If sex were a matter of technique and tickles, our society would be doing fine. The instructions are explicit; the research uninhibited; the results surely must be an explosion of properly timed orgasms all over the country.

But sex goes on between people, and somewhere in the process of sex, people keep getting in the way. The young bodies on the bed, moving to the rhythm of sex, wrapped in that very special feeling of aloneness with each other and freedom to touch, explore, penetrate and be penetrated, lie back at last alone, not with their partner now but with themslves, withdrawn into that inward vortex whose waters carry all the events of their lives, not only this one, but childhood, parents, brothers and sisters and friends and dates and dreams and realities, teachers and classmates, a skinned knee and a broken wrist, assignments and assignations, delirious victories and dreadful failures, pain and reaching out and tender arms, and the quick agony of wanting, ambitions and jobs and jealousies and bitter disappointments, and the boy next door and the girl in front of you and singing in church and flunking a test, and someone laughing at you and someone loving you,

and leaving you crying and cursing, relieved and happy
and frightened and inadequate and pretending and wondering—that inward vortex rushing down from the whirl-
ing rim to the quiet pool of self where people live—alone.
"Do you want a cigarette?"
"No thanks."
"I'll be back in a minute."
"Sure."
Who is that looking at me in the bathroom mirror? And
who is that boy waiting for me to come back and lie down
with him in the bed? And what shall I say to him?

After the flight outward and upward, and the moment
of utter release from whatever is binding and hurting, the
body withdraws—and the person is left. And history.

There is little talk about history in sex books devoted
to the Butterfly Flick and the Silken Swirl—and I won't
quarrel with any technique that makes sex more exciting.
But sex is the history of a person; it is more than tingling
and technique and release.

The sexual act of intercourse, with all its variations,
is certainly more than emphasized in our culture. But sex
is more than coupling; it is couples. It is the total history
of a man and a woman, not only driven by the desire for
sex, but also for love, tenderness, appreciation, a sense of
total freedom, a feeling of permanence, the pleasure of
giving. Driven also, it may be, by the desire for power, con-
quest, ego satisfaction, resentment, and punishment.

Sex which involves the total person is deemphasized
in our culture. If the medium is the message, then sex is
the photographer's angle in pornographic movies, the
clinical word pictures in the sex books, the Monday morning
conversation about the weekend before that I avidly listened to as a boy when I worked with grown men on construction projects in the Middle West. If the meshing of
gears and consequent disengagement of two human beings
is what sex really means, it is merely a function of the hu-

man body, exciting but without meaning other than
recreation.

H. G. Wells, a man of many sexual affairs, remarked
in his autobiographical novel, *The World of William Clis-
sold*, "I used to think that a man and a woman could meet
like a flame and part." He went on to say that he had
learned that whenever a man and a woman meet sexually,
"two worlds are altered."

So what do we tell our kids about sex? And what do
they tell us? And what distinctions, if any, do we make
between what we believe and practice, and what we want
our children to practice and believe?

More than a decade ago, when ferment about the new
morals was bursting out of articles in *Time* and *Newsweek*,
the latter published in its April 6, 1964, issue a lead
article on "Morals on the Campus"—the college campus of
course. One paragraph is significant, especially in view of
the publication of *The Feminine Mystique* the year before
and the beginning of the modern Women's Movement:

"Significantly, many young men who tout the benefits
of physical love for themselves and their dates hesitate to
say they would give their own children blanket permission
to say 'yes.' When asked whether he favored premarital
sex, one Columbia senior in turn asked, 'For me, or my kid
sister?' "

It's a good question.

I am talking to one of my clients, a sixteen-year-old
girl who is having an affair with a college boy of twenty-
one. The parents are disturbed. The girl has no intention
of giving the boy up.

"But I love him," she said, and her face lighted up.
"He's the most beautiful thing that ever happened to me."

I never forgot those words, and the warm and happy
face across the desk from me.

The boy called me on the telephone several weeks later.

"Is this Dr. Rutenber?"

"Yes, who is this?"

"You don't know me. I'm John Waters. I go with Margie Curtis. I understand you are talking to her."

"That's right."

He seemed to expect me to say more. I waited during the pause that followed.

"Look, Dr. Rutenber, I guess I'm in a little over my head."

Again the pause.

"Go ahead," I said.

"Well, the fact is that I'm very fond of Margie. She's a great kid. But I'm afraid she's gotten a little too fond of me. I'm a junior in college, you know. I plan to be a lawyer."

He seemed to feel that he had explained it all. I didn't say anything. When he spoke again, there was a note of urgency in his voice.

"You understand, don't you?"

"Why don't you tell me what you want to say?"

"She isn't pregnant," he said hopefully. "There's no problem there."

I was ready to cut it short.

"What do you want to tell me?" I snapped.

"Well, the fact is that I want to get out of this situation. I think we should stop seeing each other. After all, we can't get married or anything like that. I mean—she's awfully fond of me. I want to break it off, but I'm scared she'll commit suicide or something. Maybe you could explain it to her."

"She wouldn't believe me. She'd only call you up to get it from you. She thinks you're in love with her. Tell her yourself as gently and as quickly as you can. Her parents and I will try to pick up the pieces. Be sure her parents are home when you call. And get to it."

I warned the parents of what was coming. "Don't tell her she's been a fool," I warned. "Whatever you say don't tell her you told her so. Put your arms around her and tell her you love her and it's going to be all right. It's going to be all right. I'll be here if she wants to see me, and I hope she will, but let it come from her."

She was in my office the next morning.

"I cried most of the night," she said. "I can't cry any more. My parents were wonderful."

"I am sure they were," I said. "It's tough, I know, and it's going to take you a while to forget him, but try real hard. And don't try to win him back."

She looked at me with dry eyes.

"I feel like a used slut," she said.

One has to get back to that total picture of sexuality which is history. But history is what happened and what is happening. There is another kind of history: what could happen in the future. Potential. Sex is inevitably bound up with the potential of a person, man or woman, girl or boy. If there is a judgment working out of the essence of things, it will ask two questions of all of us. Were you sensitive to the history and the potential of people, and what did you do to understand the former and to advance the latter?

How did you use your maleness, your sex, not only in physical encounters with all of their parameters, but in your day-to-day living with your wife, your daughter, the women who work in your office, who apply to your professional schools, your banks, your businesses? To enhance their potential or to keep your own power and privileges?

How did you use your femaleness, your sex, in your day-to-day living with your husband and family, with the men in your business and professional life, with the people of both sexes with whom you came in contact, to advance them as human beings, or to ask for whatever they could give you in time and possessions and admiration?

One has to get back to that total picture of sexuality, the total person, and for this book the total teenager, with all of her and his possibilities as a human being, a boy, a girl, a man, a woman, a doctor, scientist, artist, a parent, a child, disappointed, triumphant, giving and holding back, free, joyous and fulfilled, tragic and decimated, dead with hopelessness or alive with love.

What we are trying to teach our young people about sex is an ethic of people that asks, before the situation is upon the protagonists: "Could this relationship bring the desire for permanence on her part or his that I do not have any intention or wish of fulfilling? Will the tenderness engendered by the sex act continue long after the act is completed and become a permanent emotion to my partner? And can I meet that permanent emotion or will I cut it off when it puts too closely its soft but demanding tendrils around me. Will I cause my partner pain? Can I justify this pain by the pleasure I get from the relationship?

"I feel like a used slut."

Has one a right to make another person feel this way: guilty, used, left over?

If sex is a hunger of the total person, of the emotions as well as the body, to arouse that hunger in another and then douse it like a candlelight is exploitation, dishonesty, and theft. And that goes too for the marriages that sink into torpor or light up only in angry words and self-centered demands.

We must teach a new ethic of pain that is sensitive to the unfulfilled lives of other human beings, their sense of need, their desire to be loved as persons and not merely as depositories of the coin of desire or benefactors of loneliness and the dark. There will be some who think that this extreme sensitivity to the needs and rights of others is written into the universe and enjoined in men's hearts by a graven Imperative. There will be others who will consider it the flowering of a humanism beyond the grunting ethics of "what is moral is what you feel good after." Perhaps the ultimate question is, What makes you feel good?

14 The Community of Affection

In the final chapter I do not want so much to review as to underline.

My emphasis in this book has been on the community of young people and adults, considered as one community, not two. I have not tried to construct a decalogue of rules but rather to chart the geography of a way of thinking and living which has produced unusual results.

In the first chapter, "The Second Question," I said that our philosophy was based on the answers to two questions, rather than only one: What can we, the adult world of parent, teacher, and administrator give to young people, and What can young people, our children and our students, give to the adult world? I added that the second question was rarely asked in our present society.

My final point in that chapter was that giving to the adult community presupposes a certain kind of community and certain methods of bringing up young people that make them want to give—since a gift is something bestowed and not demanded. In giving, as well as receiving, they feel needed, wanted, and appreciated. In other words, they feel loved.

The Community of Affection

So we are talking about communities of affection and mutual need in the chilly aloofness of the Age of Communication.

This is no sentimental association. I have already mentioned the rugged, abrasive quality of adult-teenage relationships. The marshmallow home exists only in sermons on Mother's Day. I have used the word "affection" rather than love. In the larger communities, affection is an easier word, though no less important. Affection is usually the public face of love, but it comes with a sense of humor and a more relaxed manner.

Affection is love in a tilted hat that can be amused at itself. It is brother to tenderness, and sister to concern. It does not demand your life, but it counts on your response and a feeling of mutual understanding and trust. Like love, whose synonym it is, it can last a lifetime. It can smile and let you go when the time comes, but its light hand on your shoulder can tighten around you in time of tragedy and failure.

The adult bears the laboring oar in the kind of community I have described. If you are going to be close to teenagers you have to forget from time to time the supposed prerogatives of adulthood, especially the machismo that hates to feel that one may need a young person. But it is only when teenagers feel needed that they want to give. It is hard to contribute to Mr. Always-in-Control-of-the-Situation or Mrs. No-One-Knows-How-to-Do-This-But-Me.

Take the case of physical labor in the home and the school. Shared physical work is one of the great builders of a sense of community, and it should start long before adolescence—as early as a child can carry silver from the table to the sink. It is especially important that this kind of work continue through the formative teen years, but this is the very time when parents tend to abdicate because of teenage opposition to working around the house and lawn without pay. Supposed fatigue or homework or dates or the telephone are all inhibitors of the urge to pitch in and help out.

But the urge to pitch in and help out is there, as the director of any institution for the retarded, hospital for crippled children, nursing home, or ghetto service can tell you. What is lacking in the home?

The parents cannot pretend to be helpless, but they can share in the work—and that includes the husband—and they can make their children realize that manual work is not something that *has* to be done, a command performance, but something that *needs* to be done, which is different.

Most independent schools have a work program. No attempt is made to dramatize this. There are no catalogue pictures of happy students with a goody-goody-give-me-a-broom look on their faces. The fact that people who live in a house help keep it clean, that people who eat at a table clean up and sweep up afterwards, should be natural and expected, and not a cause for special congratulations. But you still say thank you.

It is lamentable that the morale building value of student self-help did not strike most school and college administrators until after the maid shortage had become a national and enduring fact, but those of us who had written about the value of self-help while domestics were still at large were pleased to welcome our slower members into the club.

The Two-Way Street

I have said that the adult must bear the laboring oar in the kind of teenage-adult community I have described, but it is not a community if the adult bears the only oar. Nor will the boat progress in that fashion.

Young people need to be constantly reminded that the community makes demands on them, too. They cannot be parasites, accepting the affection and concern and trust of the community without returning those qualities themselves.

"You talk about MacDuffie being a concerned school," a girl said to me once, "but I don't agree that it is."

"Well," I said, "it's the kind of thing I can hardly prove by a diagram, but I think we are a concerned school. I certainly don't like to have anyone believe that we are not. You must have some arguments to prove your point. What are they?"

Tracy proceeded to give me several incidents where either the teachers or I seemed to her not to show concern for the students.

I argued the various cases, with no real hope of convincing her. After twenty or thirty minutes of this I said to her,

"Tracy, my next chapel talk will be an attempt to answer your question, 'Is MacDuffie a concerned school?' I hope you'll come up afterward and tell me how you liked it, and you know you don't have to agree with what I say."

"I'll be most interested," she said, "and I'll certainly come up afterward."

That Friday I announced the subject of my chapel talk: "Is MacDuffie a Concerned School?" I went on to say:

"This is a question I am asking you, and each of you knows the answer, at least for yourself. Are you concerned about the school? Are you willing to give up something for it? Are you willing to sacrifice for it? Will you support it financially when you are earning your living?

"I had an alumna once who was single and making $12,000 a year. She wrote me a letter:

Dear RDR,

I want you to know that the school changed my whole life. I am enclosing $5 for the Annual Fund.

The girls laughed, and I went on.

"Are you concerned about your fellow students? Open to their problems, trying to help them gain self-confidence and feel wanted in the school?

"Are you concerned about the faculty, the headmaster, your parents?

"Is this a concerned school?"

Tracy did not come up to see me after my talk. I managed to pass her in the dining-room.

"Hi," I said.

"Hi," she answered.

We both grinned.

The Community of Change

The kind of teenage-adult community I have tried to describe, unsentimentally, in this book is one that changes human beings at a time when they are most susceptible to change. It changes parents and teachers and headmasters, too.

Young people contribute to the inner world of the adult more than they realize. I have contended that contributions do not have to be listed: an errand, guiding a blind man across the street, sweeping the porch. These actions come out of the relationship between adults and teenagers; and this is a book about relationships.

We need to build communities

where all the clichés are on the road to oblivion;

where discipline is considered teaching;

where adults are respected and liked by teenagers because they have not abdicated their adult responsibilities;

where teenagers are respected and liked by adults because they are too mature and too close to the status of adulthood to be treated like little children;

where each generation assumes that the other wants the same kind of community, the same kind of world;

where we can get very angry with each other but never

to the point of lowering a person's self-respect, and never to the point of holding the anger beyond a brief explosion;

where the actions of young people, however deplorable, are never considered the final statement of their real character;

where both generations believe each other because of a mutual commitment to a society of truth, and an imperative to support that kind of society;

.   where the adult who tries to help build in the teenager a confidence that she is important and has a purpose to fulfill, a toughness of spirit that will enable her to rise above disappointment and defeat, and, above all, a sympathy and compassion that opens up her life to the needs of others—discovers that these qualities have in return been built up in his or her own life;

where success is measured not by money but by meaning;

where neither generation is too proud to accept and acknowledge the strength that is derived from the inescapable community of conviction and affection that they have both helped to establish in this place, at this time, with these people.

The Community We Never Leave

When Boswell asked Johnson, "Which is the more intelligent, man or woman?" the old master growled, "Which man? Which woman?"

Those of us who are confronted with a spate of books and articles on "youth" need to remember that we are not dealing with youth, but with young people.

They are not concepts in a theory; they are not statistics in a book about morals; they are not represented by any speaker or writer or publicist or politician—or parent or headmaster. They are our sons and daughters and our students. They are also themselves.

We want their best, of course, but no more. We accept

their limitations, as we accept our own. We do not consider them intellectual failures because they have failed a course or flunked out, nor do we consider them moral failures if they make serious mistakes in the world of right and wrong.

We never give up on any young person. We never say, That's all I can do, I quit. After they have left our particular community, they may surface again or we may lose track of them. Sometimes they return in strange ways.

I remember a girl who did not make the grade at MacDuffie. She had been accepted as a calculated risk. She found the work too difficult, and she didn't know how to get along with her fellow students. When she began to show signs of emotional strain, I suggested that her parents take her out in November and try to find a different kind of school. It seemed like a totally unhappy experience for her, and I felt bad about it. She was only here two months.

Four years later, during the Christmas holidays, my telephone rang at 1:00 A.M. A voice at the other end said:

"This is Janet Morris. You probably don't remember me. I was at the school for a few months in my ninth grade."

"I certainly do remember you. How are you, and what's the trouble?"

"Well, sir, I'm a senior at _____ School, and a group of us from the school are up in Vermont for a week of skiing. We just learned before we went to bed that one of our classmates was killed in an automobile accident, and we couldn't sleep, and I decided to call you, if you don't mind."

"I don't mind at all. I'm glad you called. Tell me about the girl."

She poured out the story, and I listened. There is no formula for talking about the death of a young person with all that she might have done, and become.

Janet must have talked to me for ten minutes, and I tried as well as I could to comfort her. Finally, she said:

"I feel better for talking to you, sir, but there are four freshmen who have left their rooms to stay with me because they are so upset. Could you possibly talk to them, too?"

So I talked to four complete strangers, one after the other, about the girl who had died, about their school, about themselves. It must have been close to an hour before we had finished.

"Thank you very much," Janet said at the end. "I'm so glad you didn't forget me."

There are no final grades either for the teacher or the taught—and the two roles blend—in the community we never leave. We do not have to exult that we have won or weep that we have failed. The judgment is not in our hands nor in our power of knowing. We only have to honor our commitment.

There are no commencement exercises where one can say: "There, you have received a diploma in character, summa cum laude, magna cum laude, cum laude, cum difficultate—but you have it. You have won; you are certified; go out and change the world. Temptations will bounce off you; you will not think of rationalizing your desires to still your conscience; and conscience itself will never become 'that still, small voice which tells you that someone is looking.' "

So we do not have to worry whether or not we were successful in this instance, or failed in that. We only have to ask if what we are doing is important. We think it is the most important thing in the world, and for the short time that young people are in our particular community of home or school, we are neither afraid to try to influence them nor apologetic for doing so. Influence is a two-way, three-way, four-way, four million-way street. It's the street where we all live, all the time.

Index

Adult-adolescent relationship:
growth of, from experience,
14; lack of self-consciousness
of, 13; ruggedness of, 11
Affection: community of, 218;
definition of, 218; and the
generation gap, 22; importance
of, in bringing up teenagers,
18; primacy of, in discipline,
113, 121; significance of, as
the primary value, 49
Aldridge, John W., 201
Alice in Wonderland, 44
Auden, W. H., 2

Being "pegged," 99, 123.
See also Punishment
Boyden, Frank, 17
Bunting, Mary, 42

Calderone, Mary, 208
Character: building of, through
crisis, 32; development of,
through expectation and
affection, 18-20
Community: of adults and
teenagers, 217; of affection
and mutual need, 218;
demands of, on young
people, 220; expectation of,
in creating heroism, 21-22;
expectation of, in developing
character, 18-20; formation
of, 13; greatness of, with
courage, sacrifice, and
affection, 28; of home and
school, 14; importance of
sharing physical labor in,
218-19; of influence, 224; of
mutual change, 221-22;
relationships in, 14; that we
never leave, 222-24; timidity
of, in developing teenage
ego-strength, 17-18
Concept of the heroic, 15-16;
community need for, 21-22;
and women, 16-17
Confidence building, 87
Contribution to adult
community: desire of
adolescent to give, 3-10, 13;
grows out of relationships, 10,
221; importance of thanking
adolescent for, 37-39; includes
both actions and qualities of
character, 10, 154